Higher Education in Tanzania
A Case Study

Higher Education in Africa

All titles published in association with Partnership for Higher Education in Africa

Daniel Mkude, Brian Cooksey & Lisbeth Levey
Higher Education in Tanzania
A Case Study

Nakanyike B. Musisi
& Nansozi K. Muwanga
Makerere University in Transition 1993–2000
Opportunities & Challenges

Mouzinho Mário, Peter Fry, Lisbeth Levey
& Arlindo Chilundo
Higher Education in Mozambique
A Case Study

Higher Education in Tanzania

A Case Study

Daniel Mkude
Former Chief Administrative Officer
University of Dar es Salaam

Brian Cooksey
Director
Tanzania Development Research Group

Lisbeth Levey
Director
Project for Information Access and Connectivity

*Published in association with
Partnership for Higher Education in Africa*

James Currey
OXFORD

Mkuki na Nyota
DAR ES SALAAM

Partnership for Higher Education in Africa
New York University
The Steinhardt School of Education
Department of Administration, Leadership,
and Technology
239 Greene Street
New York, New York 10011, USA

Published by

James Currey Ltd
73 Botley Road
Oxford
OX2 0BS, UK

Mkuki na Nyota
P.O. Box 4205
Dar es Salaam,
Tanzania

with the support of the Partnership for Higher Education in Africa,
an initiative of Carnegie Corporation of New York, The Ford Foundation, the John D.
and Catherine T. MacArthur Foundation, and the Rockefeller Foundation. The views
expressed are those of the authors and not necessarily the foundations that funded
this work.

1 2 3 4 5 07 06 05 04 03

British Library Cataloguing in Publication Data
Higher Education in Tanzania : a case study. - (Higher
    education in Africa)
        1. Education, Higher - Tanzania 2. Education and state -
        Tanzania 3. Universities and colleges - Tanzania
        4. Educational change - Tanzania 5. Education, Higher -
        Tanzania - Finance
        I. Mkude, Daniel   II. Cooksey, Brian   III. Levey, Lisbeth A.
        IV. Partnership for Higher Education in Africa
        378.6'78

ISBN 0-85255-425-7 Paper

Library of Congress Cataloging-in-Publication Data is available

Typeset in 11/14 Monotype Photina
by Long House Publishing Services, Cumbria, UK
Printed and bound in Britain
by Woolnough, Irthlingborough

Contents

1 Historical Background

2 The Process & Impact of Institutional Reform   15

3 The Ingredients of Institutional Transformation   31

4 Economic, Political & Educational Sector Transformations   55

Appendices

List of Tables

List of Boxes

List of Acronyms

AVU	African Virtual University
BRALUP	Bureau of Resource Assessment and Land Use Planning
BERE	Bureau of Educational Research and Evaluation
BICO	Bureau for Industrial Cooperation
CACO	Chief Academic Officer
CADO	Chief Administrative Officer
CCM	Chama Cha Mapinduzi (Tanzania ruling party)
DARUSO	Dar es Salaam University Students' Organization
DRP	Directorate of Research and Publications
ERB	Economic Research Bureau
FASS	Faculty of Arts and Social Sciences
FCM	Faculty of Commerce and Management
FDI	foreign direct investment
FOE	Faculty of Engineering
FOEd	Faculty of Education
FOL	Faculty of Law
GTZ	German Agency for Technical Cooperation
HEAC	Higher Education Accreditation Council
HIPC	Highly Indebted Poor Country
ICT	Information and Communications Technologies
IDS	Institute of Development Studies
IFI	International Financial Institution
IGU	Income Generating Unit
IRA	Institute of Resource Assessment
ITP	Institutional Transformation Programme
LAN	Local Area Network
MOEC	Ministry of Education and Culture
MOH	Ministry of Health
MSTHE	Ministry of Science, Technology and Higher Education
MUCHS	Muhimbili University College of Health Sciences
NGO	Non-governmental organization
NORAD	Norwegian Agency for Development Cooperation
NUFFIC	Netherlands Organization for Cooperation in Higher Education

NUFU	Norwegian Council for Higher Education Programme for Development Research and Education
OUT	Open University of Tanzania
PMU	Programme Management Unit
SAREC	SIDA Department for Research Cooperation
SDC	Swiss Agency for Development Cooperation
SIDA	Swedish International Development Cooperation Agency
SUA	Sokoine University of Agriculture
TADREG	Tanzania Development Research Group
UCB	University Consultancy Bureau
UCLAS	University College of Lands and Architectural Studies
UDASA	University of Dar es Salaam Staff Association
UDSM	University of Dar es Salaam
URT	United Republic of Tanzania
USARF	University Students' African Revolutionary Front
USHEPIA	University Science, Humanities and Engineering Partnerships in Africa

Preface to the Series

The Partnership for Higher Education in Africa began as an affirmation of the ability of African universities to transform themselves and promote national development. We, the presidents of four US foundations – Carnegie Corporation of New York, The Ford Foundation, the John D. and Catherine T. MacArthur Foundation and the Rockefeller Foundation – came together out of a common belief in the future of African universities. Our interest in higher education proceeds from a simple faith that an independent scholarly community supported by strong universities goes hand-in-hand with a healthy, stable democracy. Universities are vitally important to Africa's development. Their crucial activities in research, intellectual leadership and developing successive generations of engaged citizens will nourish social, political and economic transformation in Africa. By pooling our resources, the foundations will help advance the reform of African universities and accelerate the development of their countries.

Much of sub-Saharan Africa has suffered deep stagnation over the last two decades and is staggering under the weight of domestic and international conflict, disease (especially the plague of HIV/AIDS), poverty, corruption and natural disasters. Its universities – once shining lights of intellectual excitement and promise – suffered from an enormous decline in government resources for education. In the last half of the last decade, however, things began to change in a number of countries. Our interest was captured by the renewal and resurgence that we saw in several African nations and at their universities, brought about by stability, democratization, decentralization and economic liberalization. Within these universities a new generation of leadership has stepped forward to articulate a vision for their institutions, inspiring confidence among those who care about African higher education. The case studies found that while the universities represented in these volumes have widely varying contexts and traditions, they are engaged in broad reform: examining and revising their planning processes, introducing new techniques of financial management, adopting new technologies, reshaping course structures and pedagogy and reforming practices of governance.

The first three case studies, on Makerere University and on the systems of higher education in Mozambique and Tanzania, focus on three of the six sub-Saharan countries that the Partnership has selected for concentration: Ghana, Mozambique, Nigeria, South Africa, Tanzania and Uganda. These six were chosen because their universities were initiating positive change, developing a workable planning process and demonstrating genuine commitment to national capacity building, in contexts of national reform.

The studies commissioned by the Partnership were carried out under the leadership of local scholars, using a methodology that incorporates feedback from the institutions under study and involving a broad range of stakeholders.

The publication of the first three case studies in this series is closely in line with the major aims of the Partnership:

- generating and sharing information about African universities and higher education
- supporting universities seeking to transform themselves
- enhancing research capacity on higher education in Africa
- promoting collaboration among African researchers, academics and university administrators

The studies are the product of the foundations' support for conceptual work that generates information about African higher education and university issues. Through the case studies, the foundations hope to promote a wider recognition of the importance of universities to African development. Additional studies will be published in late 2003, together with an essay on crosscutting themes from the case studies.

The foundations together have contributed $62.3 million

through December 2001, to fund higher education reform efforts in the targeted countries and institutions involved. The conceptual work supported by the individual foundations, working together in partnership towards a common vision, seeks to ensure the strengthening of institutional capacity for research on higher education in Africa and the wide dissemination of African research output.

We hope that the publication of these case studies will help advance the state of knowledge about higher education in Africa and support the movement for university reform on the continent. Equally significant, the process of our involvement in the case studies has enhanced our own understanding and helped the foundations focus future efforts of the Partnership. Interest in higher education in Africa has grown since the Partnership was launched in 2000. In this way, the Partnership not only uses its own resources but also acts as a catalyst to generate the support of others, on the continent and elsewhere, for African universities as vital instruments for development. We see these case studies as a critical step in the process of regeneration and transformation.

Vartan Gregorian, President
CARNEGIE CORPORATION OF NEW YORK

Susan Berresford, President
THE FORD FOUNDATION

Jonathan Fanton, President
JOHN D. AND CATHERINE T. MACARTHUR FOUNDATION

Gordon Conway, President
ROCKEFELLER FOUNDATION

Acknowledgements

The authors would like to thank all those who have helped in the preparation of this report. Josephine Kimaro served ably as our research assistant. Professor T. Mbwette of the Programme Implementation Unit and his staff greatly facilitated the data collection exercise. Interviews were held with the Vice-Chancellor of UDSM, Professor M. Luhanga, the Vice-Chancellor of OUT, Professor G. Mmari, Professors S. Chachage (FASS), A. Ishumi (FOEd), I. Kikula (IRA), I. Kimambo (History), G. Malekela (FoEd), A. Mascarenhas (IRA), J. R. Mashua, (FOE), L. Msambichaka (ERB), R.S. Mukandala (Dean, FASS), B. Mutagahywa (Computer Centre), M.H.H. Nkunya, (CACO), Chris Peter (FOL) and Drs A. S. Chungu (Income Generating Unit), C. C. Joseph (Department of Chemistry), M.M. Kissaka (Department of Electrical Engineering), A. Lwaitama (FASS), E. Kaijage (FCM), Y. D. Mgaya (Zoology), K. Osaki (FOEd), H. Sosovele (IRA), J. Lindstrom (SIDA), E. Masanja, (Department of Chemical and Process Engineering), Y. Mshana (African Virtual University), J. Nawe (Main Library) and R. Avenstrup (Roaven Educational), Dr Andrew Temu, S. Noah, Michael Wort, Seamus Heaney (Ministry of Education and Culture), Victor de la Torre (European Union Delegation), and William Sabaya (HEAC). In addition, the principals of MUCHS, Professor Jacob Mtabaji, and UCLAS, Professor Alpheo Nikundiwe, kindly took time off from their busy schedules for a productive work session.

1 Historical Background

The first decade

The University of Dar es Salaam (UDSM) was first established in 1961 as a college of the University of London. In 1963, it became a constituent college of the University of East Africa, and in 1970 an independent national university, along with the other constituent colleges of Nairobi and Makerere. To demonstrate its commitment to university education, the then ruling party, the Tanganyika African National Union (TANU), offered its newly built headquarters along Lumumba Street in Dar es Salaam for use by the young University College until the latter could secure its own premises. After a massive mobilization of local and foreign resources, in 1964 the college was able to move to its own magnificent buildings on Observation Hill, 16 kilometres northwest of the city centre.

When the college became an independent national university, the Head of State became its titular head as Chancellor. It is argued that this twinning of roles was responsible for giving university issues a high profile in national politics, sometimes with dire consequences. Convinced that the university was a strategic weapon in the fight against poverty, ignorance and disease, political leaders made strong efforts to draw it into government centralized planning, to the point of dictating admission conditions. A telling example of this is the Musoma Resolution of 1974, which directed that students were eligible for higher education only if they had completed one year of compulsory national service and had a minimum of two years' satisfactory work experience and positive recommendations from employers.

This was a radical departure from the practice that had prevailed at the university in the first ten years of independence. The university system then operated along lines similar to universities elsewhere in the British Commonwealth. Admission was chiefly based on 'Advanced' level performance, while courses and programmes were designed and packaged similarly to other Commonwealth universities. The academic

1

year was divided into three terms, each of about 10–11 weeks duration each. Academic progress was measured chiefly by term papers and end-of-year examinations. Although the university depended totally on the government for funding, it was relatively free in determining admission conditions, course content and structure, as well as modalities of assessment.

After 1970: UDSM as a developmental university

The Musoma Resolution was just one of several measures taken in the early 1970s that tied the university to the development path and ideology of the state. The appointment of a former executive secretary of the ruling party to the post of Vice-Chancellor is another example of the attempt to institutionalize party control over the day-to-day affairs of the university. Besides directives to review curricula to make them relevant to the needs and aspirations of the people of Tanzania, there were also efforts to establish new units specifically charged with addressing particular development issues. The Economic Research Bureau (ERB), Bureau of Resource Assessment and Land Use Planning (BRALUP, the present Institute of Resource Assessment), the Institute of Kiswahili Research and the Institute of Adult Education all came into existence in this way.

Some of these efforts were commendable because they challenged the university community to link organically with the broader society and identify itself with its needs and aspirations. A course called 'Development Studies' was also introduced and made compulsory for all first- and second-year students. The general aims of this course were:

• to expose students to the theories and problems of social development in the third world in general and in Africa and Tanzania in particular;

- to guide students to an understanding of alternative development strategies at both national and international levels;
- to enable students to develop appropriate tools for analysing and resolving development issues as they related to their specific disciplines.

Field attachment or practical training was already an integral part of professional courses, such as education and engineering. In an attempt to merge theory with practice and in order to shake off the 'ivory tower' image, the field attachment was extended to all disciplines. The purposes of the attachment programmes were:

- to enable students to apply theory to solving real-life problems;
- to give students an opportunity to acquire appropriate work experience to complement their academic training;
- to establish close contact between employers and the faculties for mutual benefit.

Between the late 1960s and mid-1970s, the University of Dar es Salaam acquired a reputation for scholarship that espoused causes and issues related to liberation, social justice and economic development.

According to Shivji (1993), in the period 1967–75 the university developed into one of the best known universities in Africa, if not the world. During this period the campus was immersed in one of the most vigorous debates that have taken place in Tanzania in the wake of the Arusha Declaration and the Mwongozo Guidelines. The original initiators of this process were students, through their organization, the University Students' African Revolutionary Front (USARF), and later, the TANU Youth League. Their mouthpiece was their journal *Cheche*, which within a short period of time acquired an international reputation for its scholarly excellence as well as commitment.

Genuine attempts were made to shape the university as an instrument of development. Reflecting upon what had happened at the University of Dar es Salaam during this period, Ajayi et al. (1996) conclude: 'Dar es Salaam soon became known as the prototype of the Developmental University truly responsive to its society.'

Unrest & attempts at reform

Measures to reorganize the university to make it responsive to the needs and aspirations of the people of Tanzania were not always well received. On two occasions, they sparked off student protests. In 1966, 223 students were expelled for demonstrating against compulsory national service, which had been introduced to curb elitist tendencies and inculcate graduates with a sense of public service. In 1971, soon after Dar es Salaam became an independent national university, students decided to protest against what they considered oppressive new structures being introduced by the administration led by the newly appointed Vice-Chancellor. This protest, known as the Akivaga crisis, took the form of boycotts and sit-ins and lasted a long time. It was eventually decided that the new Vice-Chancellor had been over-zealous and out of step with the established procedures of the university.

These two events gave rise to conflicting interpretations. One interpretation maintains that these were manifestations of resistance to the move to drive higher education by outdated, authoritarian development ideologies. Another point of view, championed by Shivji and others, views the incidents as protests against incipient bureaucratization invading the university: 'The democratic process was born in the womb of the student struggles of the late '60s culminating in the Akivaga crisis of 1971.' (Shivji, 1993: 66)

The Akivaga crisis precipitated two important developments whose repercussions are still visible even today.

- The Mungai Committee that investigated the crisis recommended the installation of formal democratic structures at the university. This took the form of a proliferation of committees on which staff and students were represented. Thus the University of Dar es Salaam's reputation for participatory representation on numerous committees had its roots in the crisis.
- During the crisis academic staff realized that without an organization and a forum of their own they were vulnerable. They therefore demanded to form an academic assembly of their own, for which permission was granted ten years later. This is the origin of the University of Dar es Salaam Staff Association (UDASA).

After the crises, both staff and students tended to see the new university administration as a threat to their cherished democratic principles and values. In 1971 the university authorities banned both the USARF publication *Cheche* and USARF itself.

The crisis deepens

The economic problems that Tanzania experienced after the mid-1970s compounded the soured relationship between the university administration and staff, on the one hand, and the students, on the other. The collapse of the East African Community, the war against Idi Amin, the support for liberation struggles near and far, poor economic policies and the crisis in the world economy meant a sharp decline in university resources.

Three significant events led to a worsening of internal relations within the university in the late 1970s. In 1977, some five Tanzanian academics were arbitrarily 'retired in the public interest'. In 1978, 350 students were expelled for demonstrating against the increase in privileges that Members of Parliament had just voted for themselves. In 1979, contracts of some 16 expatriate lecturers were not renewed, for

5

reasons that were unclear. It was speculated that this might be a way of curbing the spread of progressive or unorthodox ideas at the Hill, as the university was called.

The 1980s: decade of decline

Economic woes and soured internal relations combined to produce a depressing mood in the university community during the 1980s. Shivji (1993: 83) captures it well:

The present malaise of the university has been variously described by different commentators in reports and other writings. However, all of them are agreed on one thing: that there is something wrong and that different sections of the university community are labouring under deep-seated grievances, discontent and generally low morale and spirits.

According to Shivji, some of the symptoms of the disease that affected the university were:

- apathy
- neglect of the welfare of staff and students
- lack of consultation
- unilateral decision-making
- bureaucratic inefficiency and red tape
- bureaucratic domination

The last three elements, which were the most frequently cited in discussions and debates, were held responsible for the prevalence of the first two. A strong sense of resentment developed between the staff and students, on the one hand, and the administration on the other. Even the Macha Report of 1979 identified lack of democracy and bureaucratic domination as the causes for the breakdown of communication within the community:

It was claimed that the breakdown in communication was a reflection of a two-fold trend, which has characterized and has become dominant at the university. First was the lack of democratic discussion/debate in decision making. Second was the bureaucratic dominance over decision-making processes, especially committees that were dominated by the administrators. (Macha, 1979: 7)

During this period the focus of debates shifted from development issues to power politics. Shivji (1993: 85) notes that 'Unlike the debates in the 'sixties and 'seventies, the debates of the '80s were not always situated firmly within an anti-imperialist ideology nor guided by a grand theory of society'.

Financial crisis

The economic woes that began in the late 1970s escalated throughout the 1980s. Books and other teaching materials and equipment, along with many other goods in the country, became rare commodities. The overall impact on the teaching-learning process was profound. Table 1 summarizes the recurrent subventions to UDSM from 1984 to 2000.

UDSM's total funds as well as funds per student fell by nearly two-thirds during the period 1984–93, close to the average for sub-Saharan Africa (Saint, 1992: xii). As the number of students remained stable, UDSM avoided the negative impact on quality associated with rapidly rising enrolments.

While student and academic staff numbers were more or less constant during this period, there was a 14 per cent increase in non-academic staff. However, since 1995–6 non-academic staff numbers have decreased by 55 per cent, a dramatic turnaround by any standard. Academic staff numbers have fallen by a fifth since 1986, whereas student numbers have increased by over 60 per cent during the same period.

As a result of inflation, the total value of salaries fell by 47 per cent during the decade. Nevertheless, the wages and

7

Table 1: Main campus operating budget & unit expenditures, 1984–5 to 1999–2000

	Operating budget (US$m)	Number of students	Academic staff	Non-academic staff	Student cost per head (US$)
1984/5	22.8	2,913	680	1,715	7,824
1985/6	18.8	2,987	715	1,765	6,302
1986/7	14.6	2,972	726	1,685	4,914
1987/8	8.5	2,891	664	1,863	2,924
1988/9	8.4	2,743	678	1,727	3,078
1989/90	9.5	2,839	675	1,798	3,346
1990/91[a]	11.0	–	685	1,847	3,316
1991/2	15.9	2,801	689	1,924	5,689
1992/3	11.5	2,992	692	1,966	3,850
1993/4	6.6	2,968	681	1,953	2,752
1994/5	15.3	2,951	614	2,012	2,242
1995/6	7.8	3,544	601	2,012	2,199
1996/7	10.3	3,770	578	1,297	2,726
1997/8	10.7	4,131	594	1,230	2,586
1998/9	11.0	4,172	581	1,224	2,632
1999/2000	15.6	4,816	579	898	3,236

Sources: UDSM 1995b, 12–13; *Facts and Figures 1999/2000*: 10, 23–4.
Note: a) In 1990–1 UDSM was closed for the entire academic year.

salaries bill grew rapidly as a proportion of total spending, from 39 per cent of the recurrent budget in 1992 to 65 per cent in 1996 (URT, MSTHE, 1998). Other budget items, including staff development, office stationery and examination expenses, fell from 49 per cent of recurrent expenditure to 30 per cent during the same period, seriously affecting the quality of teaching and learning.

The donors' share of development expenditure grew from 65 per cent in 1984 to 92 per cent in 1993.

Groping for solutions: the genesis of ITP

If the 1980s were a decade of decline, then the 1990s can be described as a decade of groping for solutions. Between 1988 and 1993, the university witnessed five major developments that played a catalytic role in ushering in the process that gave birth to the Institutional Transformation Programme (ITP):

- In 1988, for the first time in the history of the university, a career academic, Professor Geoffrey Mmari, was appointed Vice-Chancellor. All his predecessors had had strong political affiliations but no serious academic grounding.
- The Faculty of Engineering embarked on a transformation programme that sent ripples through the rest of the university.
- In 1990–1, the university was closed for eight months (the academic year) following violent student riots, sparked off by dissatisfaction over welfare matters and the government's poor handling of them.
- In late 1990, another academic was appointed chief administrative officer (CADO). This move resulted in the academics holding the three top leadership positions. Previously the only top post held by an academic was that of chief academic officer (CACO).
- In 1991, there was a reshuffle in the top two leadership positions.

From 1989 to 1991, numerous analyses, studies and reports were commissioned in an attempt to understand the nature of the problems afflicting the university. From January 1991, a comprehensive review and analysis of all previous studies resulted in a document entitled the *Management Effectiveness*

Review Report. This was followed by a series of workshops aimed at creating a broad awareness of the nature of the problems afflicting the university and arriving at a consensus on what should be done to overcome these problems. General and sectoral strengths, weaknesses, opportunities and risks were discussed within a wide spectrum of national and international references and experiences. There was a general realization that the university had accumulated numerous internal weaknesses at a time when its mission, objectives and functions were challenged by other institutions in the country and in the region.

Moreover, as a result of national and global economic crises, the resource flow from government to the university was drastically reduced, as described below. As the discussions deepened, it became clear that the malaise afflicting the university had seeped so deeply into its institutional fabric that a piecemeal approach would not provide an adequate solution. It was therefore decided that the best approach was to systematically overhaul the entire institution. The process of implementing this momentous decision was code-named the 'UDSM 2000 Transformation Programme'.

Role of the Faculty of Engineering (FOE)

The Faculty of Engineering was established after most of the other faculties. The young FOE soon realized that its efforts to consolidate what it had achieved in the relatively short period of ten years or so was being threatened by an economic crisis and reduced resource flows. Newly trained staff in whom the faculty and donors had invested heavily became frustrated and left for greener pastures.

Professor Masuha, dean of the faculty, ordered an in-depth review of the activities of the faculty. The review found that the core issue was inadequate remuneration, forcing academic staff to seek other employment or engage in 'PESA' (Personal Economic Survival Activities).[1]

10

The university decided to devise a strategy to help curb this trend. At an internal workshop in 1989 various strategies were agreed upon and supported by the faculty's traditional donors, Germany (GTZ) and Switzerland (SDC). The plan almost hived off the faculty from the rest of the university, as it sought to make it as autonomous and self-sufficient as possible. Issues covered in the plan included cost control, performance monitoring and evaluation, staff retention, financing undergraduate and postgraduate programmes, research and technological development, and consultancy.

One of the features that captured the attention of people outside the FOE was the introduction of performance-based incentive schemes. To some extent, the FOE has served as a schooling ground for strategic planning and change management for staff in other parts of the university. It certainly provided inspiration for the larger reform process.

The faculty had built a solid foundation for engineering studies. In a recent comparative regional study of faculties of engineering at five different universities in the region, Dar es Salaam ranked first, followed by the University of Zimbabwe. According to the report:

The measures taken by University of Dar es Salaam (Faculty of Engineering) to stabilize its academic staff are worth noting and using as model for other faculties of engineering. These include:

- establishment of the Bureau for Industrial Cooperation (BICO), through which academic staff can provide consulting, technical and continuing education services to industry and thereby beef up their incomes;
- emphasis on enrolment of young staff members in sandwich Ph.D. (rather than full-time overseas) programmes with facilitation and incentives to ensure that staff are able to complete their studies within reasonable time and without undue stress;
- introduction of a flexible research fund to enable staff (particularly young staff who just completed doctoral studies) to do research and publish the results;

11

• Introduction of clear and transparent policies and procedures on all key functions of the faculty, including workload monitoring, to insure adequate compensation for those with excessive workloads. (SIDA, 1999)

External stimuli to the reform process

Although the impulse and initiative for reform came from within, there is no doubt that donors played a significant role in facilitating the conceptualization, planning and implementation of the reform process at UDSM in a number of ways.

Whereas the FOE could ask GTZ to fund the initial planning processes of reform, at the university-wide level there was no obvious donor to turn to for resources. SIDA/SAREC volunteered to provide flexible funding to enable the university to undertake the initial steps of planning and setting up a reform process. At about the same time, NORAD and GTZ began to express concern about the sustainability of their investments in the Faculty of Science (notably in the Departments of Chemistry and of Chemical and Process Engineering). The realization that islands of excellence had been created, resulting in a capable institutional framework that could protect and promote their interests, prompted NORAD and GTZ to take a keen interest in the emerging reform process.

GTZ offered to fund the reform of the financial system, which was at the top of the agenda. At the same time, NORAD began discussions with the university about moving away from funding individual departments to providing flexible funds to the institution as a whole, with an understanding of how they would be used. The concept of the frame agreement emerged in this way. In 1997, in the first frame agreement to be signed, NORAD became the first donor to accept the university's strategic plan as the basis for formulating its assistance. The agreement with NORAD covered a broad spectrum of activities intended to increase institutional capacity and enhance professional standards, with the university mandated to do the detailed planning, implementation, accounting and reporting.

The units that had traditionally benefited from these donors were a little wary and apprehensive of the frame agreement approach. Both the university and the donors had to assure them that this was not a ploy to abandon them but rather a strategy to strengthen the institutional base of their achievements.

Both national and international environments stimulated the reform process. Nationally, one can identify political and socio-economic factors that were able to influence the reform process.[2] Although the one-party state has been peacefully dismantled in recent years, many of the main actors from earlier days still occupy senior leadership positions in government and the ruling party continues to enjoy a relatively comfortable majority in Parliament. Internal checks and balances in government remain few. Vested interests in the status quo and fear of rapid change underlie the reluctance of the state to loosen central control of economic and social activities, including higher education.

On the other hand, concern with the ever-increasing knowledge gap between the economically developed and less developed parts of the world has provided a tremendous stimulus to change.[3] Tanzania's President Mkapa stated in the 1999 *Progress Report*:

Recognizing that the world of the 21st century will increasingly be globalized, we must devise new and more stringent strategies in initiating and managing change in African universities. Of necessity, African universities will have to strive to improve further the quality of their output if they are to continue to maintain even their current share of the local and international labour market. (UDSM, 2000a: 27)

In key areas, the national Civil Service Reform Programme,

introduced in 1992, had a very important demonstration effect on the Institutional Transformation Programme (ITP), effectively countering resistance to change within UDSM. Downsizing the central government establishment, redefining the role of the public service and introducing meritocratic recruitment and performance-based management all served to lend support to the principles of the ITP, including the difficult component of retrenchment of administrative staff.

Contacts with regional, continental & international organizations

During the early 1990s when the reform process was taking shape, the university made contact with the Association of African Universities which, in conjunction with such organizations as the Economic Commission for Africa and UNESCO, had been organizing seminars and workshops to address specific problems facing African universities. UDSM participated eagerly in these meetings whenever funding was available. The exchanges underlined the importance of the critical role played by leadership in any process of change, and the need to develop alternative sources of funding. In the course of these meetings, the university made contact with three South African institutions: the Centre for Higher Education Transformation (CHET), the South African Association of Institutional Research (SAAIR) and University Science, Humanities and Engineering Partnerships in Africa (USHEPIA), from which it obtained ideas useful to the reform process.

Notes

1   The word *pesa* in Swahili means money.
2   Trends in the political arena in Tanzania are described in Chapter 4.
3   UDSM's *Rolling Strategic Plan* provides a clear expression of the survival imperative in the global knowledge society. UDSM/PMU, *University-level Five-Year Rolling Strategic Plan, 1997–2002* (UDSM, 1997), p. 8.

2 The Process & Impact of Institutional Reform

Objectives of the ITP

The immediate objectives of the ITP were threefold:

- to achieve a broad awareness of institutional facts and figures, strengths, weaknesses, opportunities and risks;
- to achieve a consensus on the corporate mission, objectives, strategic plan, policies and logistics of the university;
- to pursue an institutional development process leading to an organization that valued scholarship, rational dialogue and consensual relationships.

The overall objective was to carry out strategic long-term reform that would enable the university to overcome its weaknesses and equip it to meet challenges and fulfil its role in the twenty-first century.

Strategic planning

Following the decision to embark upon a process of self-renewal and reform, the university undertook two tasks to lay a firm foundation for the programme's implementation, namely: gathering data on the university in order to give the community a broad awareness of its strengths and weaknesses; and drafting a corporate strategic plan to guide the reform process.

After intensive discussions and consultations, the University Council approved the Corporate Strategic Plan of 1993 in August 1994. The document, which touches on all aspects of the institution, covers the basic concepts, aspirations, goals, objectives and philosophy underlying the envisaged reform process. Its five sub-themes are:

- mission, objectives and functioning;
- corporate set-up (ownership, autonomy, governance and administrative structures);

15

- inputs (management styles, policies, planning, finance, back-up services, personnel and student welfare);
- outputs (principles underpinning academic activities such as undergraduate and postgraduate studies, research and consultancy).

Although the plan was not prepared by planning professionals, it accurately captured the sentiments and wishes of a broad spectrum of people concerned about the future of the institution. The document asserts that, in order for the institution to produce capable, dependable and marketable outputs, it would have to undergo major surgery in its corporate set-up and inputs. In addition to the adoption of the strategic plan, the first *Facts and Figures* was published in 1995 and has been updated annually ever since.

As originally conceived, the reform process was to run for 15 years, from 1993 to 2008. However, the concept of a five-year strategic plan was adopted in order to monitor progress on a regular basis and adjust course if necessary. In July 1996 a companion document to the strategic plan, the *University-Level Five-Year Rolling Strategic Plan*, was issued to guide faculties, institutes and departments in preparing their own five-year rolling strategic and operational plans. In the preface to this document, Vice-Chancellor Luhanga stated that 'Both the corporate and the five-year strategic plan will be regularly reviewed and updated to match the rapidly changing environment' (UDSM, 1996: ii).

The *Five-Year Rolling Strategic Plan* shows clearly the achievements that the university was seeking and how it intended to realize them. The document enunciates 15 strategic objectives covering a broad range of institutional life, each followed by a battery of strategies and activities to be used. However, the objectives are rather general and the strategies/ activities leading to their realization are sometimes disjointed and poorly aligned.

16

Since 1998, the faculties and institutes have also been producing their own five-year rolling plans modelled on the university-wide five-year rolling strategic plan. These concentrate on matters relating to what the Corporate Strategic Plan refers to as the input and output divisions – elements, processes and issues closely tied up with, or directly impacting the academic process. Semi-annual workshops are held to review progress in the implementation of the plan.

New governance & management structures

Three instruments were created, namely, the Steering Committee, the Programme Management Unit (PMU), and the Annual Consultative Meeting which brings together all stakeholders, including donor agencies, to coordinate and give concrete shape to the implementation process. The Steering Committee has six members, namely, the Vice-Chancellor (chairperson), Chief Academic Officer, Chief Administrative Officer, Dean of Commerce and Management, Dean of the Faculty of Education and the Manager of the Programme Management Unit (as Secretary). Its terms of reference are:

- to ensure the setting up and adequate functioning of the PMU;
- to appoint members of the Programme Management Team and define their terms of reference;
- to receive, discuss and give advice and directives on reports from the PMU;
- to discuss and approve financial reports, budgets and operational requirements of the programme submitted by the PMU;
- to decide and direct on submissions to relevant university organs, units or committees;
- to monitor and direct university external relations and cooperation related to the programme activities. (UDSM, ITP, 1995: 9).

17

The Programme Management Unit was charged with the following:

• planning, setting up and monitoring task forces and studies pertinent to the reform process;
• identifying and deploying internal and external consultants and advisers for the process;
• promoting the programme internally and externally;
• mobilizing financial, physical and human resources needed for the programme;
• monitoring the gradual transfer of reform activities into regular UDSM structures and offices.

State–university relations

The Corporate Strategic Plan raised two issues relating to questions of governance and funding that require state approval. Both were the subject of intense debate during the first years of the university-wide rolling plan. The 1970 Act establishing the University of Dar es Salaam lacks the kind of flexibility and adaptability the university needs in order to adjust to rapid changes. After intense dialogue and deliberation, a new act is in preparation which seeks to transfer powers of control from the government to the University Council and from the Council to decentralized centres of responsibility such as colleges and faculties.

On the question of funding, the programme envisages a move away from a budget based on annual grants from the government to one based on unit costs. The university carried out a computation of unit costs and found them to be very high. This prompted it to look again at its running costs in order to cut down on waste. Since 1997–8, the Council has insisted on preparing the annual budget on a unit-cost basis. The government has stated that it is prepared to accept the principle of unit costing but is not yet willing to adopt it for one institution alone.

UDSM Commitment to the ITP

The internal constituency at UDSM in favour of the ITP consists of a sizeable segment of the staff, both academic and non-academic, and students. Traditionally, many academic staff and students tended to view the university administration as an extension of the government and party control. The demise of one-party hegemony saw the end of attempts to absorb the university into a uniform political programme. But the state still retains a strong impulse towards political and bureaucratic control of what goes on at 'the Hill', coloured, no doubt, by the history of periodic conflict between the university (both students and staff) and the country's previous leaders.

Academic staff

In general, senior staff give the university administration credit for its proactive approach to securing greater autonomy for the university. UDASA sees its role as lobbying for good governance in its own relations with administration and students and defending academic staff interests in general as well as 'the social conscience of Tanzanian society' (Chacage, quoted by Masabo, 2000: 5).

UDASA has supported the ITP from the outset. According to Tumbo Masabo, efforts have been made to encourage all staff to become involved in the implementation of the UDSM transformation programme (*ibid*). UDASA's views on the reform process are contained in the so-called 'Kaijage Report', which reviews the ITP (Kaijage, 1993). The Association's position is that 'Only change that strengthens democratization processes and enhances the adoption of organic as opposed to mechanical modes of organization behaviour can be sustained'. UDASA proposed to monitor the programme to detect undesirable effects in order to 'eliminate them in good time'. It claims that the Treasury's adoption of a pay package for academics was based on its own proposals, subsequently

19

Box 1: Deans, directors & democracy at UDSM

Until 1997, deans, directors and departmental heads at UDSM were appointed through democratic elections. In 1997, the University Council voted to drop the elective principle in favour of a procedure involving a search committee. Campaigning for posts was banned.

The University Staff Assembly (UDASA) feels this decision was taken without adequate consultation with academic staff members.

The new procedure was launched after accusations of irregularities in the appointment of deans in the Faculty of Arts and Social Sciences (FASS), Faculty of Education (FOEd) and FOE in 1997. Investigations found that the irregularities, including vote buying and tribalism, were largely unfounded and possibly fabricated by disgruntled staff members. Rerunning the elections in FASS resulted in the same candidate winning.

UDASA are now campaigning for the reintroduction of the elective principle on the grounds that the search committee procedure is undemo-cratic and 'could easily put the selection of leaders into the hands of a magic circle of cronies'. Replacing the elective principle by the search committee would mean 'long term damage to the University's good image as the pace setter in the on-going democratization process'.

Source: *UDASA Newsletter* 10, 1 (March 2000), pp. 2–4.

---

endorsed by the Committee of Vice-Chancellors and Principals (1995–8).

In spite of UDASA's overall support for the ITP, some senior staff distrust the administration's commitment to more demo-cratic governance of university affairs in the new era of 'trans-parency and accountability'. In regard to the elective principle for the selection of departmental office holders (see Box 1), UDASA argues that:

The University of Dar es Salaam as a hub of higher learning in the country should set an example of good governance, and it could contribute greatly to the democratization process in the country by continuing to perfect the elective principle in harmony with the spirit of the times (UDASA, 1997).

Students

In a country with a minute higher education sector (less than 20,000 out of a population of 30 million), university students are inevitably prone to an elitist self-image. The universal tendency for educational attainments to reflect the advantages and disadvantages of social background may serve to reinforce these elitist tendencies (see below).

Until recently, the majority of graduates ended up working for the government or the state corporations (parastatals). Though salaries were appallingly low, there was job security and, sometimes, considerable advantages to be gained from working in the state apparatus, including opportunities for postgraduate studies.

The transition to the market economy has radically undermined these well-established arrangements, and the ITP reflects the imperative for change that this transition implies. Little is known, however, about how students view their future life chances and work opportunities. The following story (Box 2) demonstrates that an elitist self-image still prevails, at least among engineering students.

As part of their induction into UDSM, students are exposed to the content and rationale behind the ITP. They are told that facilities are cramped because UDSM is expanding rapidly, and lecture rooms must be shared between faculties.[1] Whether the FOE students were articulating other unstated grievances or simply protecting their own privileges (engineers are said to look down on arts, law and social science students as studying inferior disciplines) is not known.

Box 2: Uncivil engineers

On Friday 7 April 2000, violence erupted in and around lecture room A21 between some second-year civil engineering students and third-year law students who were sitting for an examination ... During the violence some university officials were mishandled, some students who were lawfully using the lecture room were beaten up, some of them sustained bodily injuries, and a lot of damage was done to university property.

On the afternoon of the same day, engineering students held an unauthorized assembly at the Faculty of Engineering ... the same engineering students, without seeking permission, marched to the ... administration building, conducted a sit-in demonstration outside the building and the Council Chamber instilling fear and preventing university employees from carrying out their normal duties.

On the evening of the same day engineering students occupied the plaza of the engineering complex and denied access to students of mathematics and their lecturer who had a scheduled lecture.

On Thursday, 13 April, the Vice-Chancellor issued a press release announcing the suspension of all second-year civil engineering students and directing them to vacate the main campus by 4 p.m.

For demonstrating solidarity with the second-year students, all engineering undergraduates were promptly suspended. Most were subsequently reinstated on declaring that they were fully in favour of the principle of sharing university facilities. The university administration subsequently prosecuted fifteen leaders of the engineering students for instigating violence and the destruction of property.

Source: UDSM Advertisement, *Daily News* (19 April 2000).

Administrative staff

The university's administrative staff might appear to be among the major losers from the ITP, since concerns about the efficiency of management at UDSM have led to major retrenchments, both directly (staff reductions) and indirectly (privatizing peripheral services).

The trade union that caters for the interests of workers at the university, and other institutions of higher education, is the Researchers, Academicians and Allied Workers' Union (RAAWU). It has a branch at the university with a membership of about 400 workers. The majority of these are support staff – allied workers rather than researchers or academicians. Researchers and academicians tend to shun this trade union, which is often portrayed as a union of workers against the educated class, including the management.

Although in theory the RAAWU branch has all along supported the ITP, in practice it has had serious misgivings with regard to any measures that entail reduction or retrenchment of staff. However, because massive retrenchment is an integral part of the Civil Service Reform Programme, the union reluctantly agreed to swallow the bitter pill as aimed at restoring economic rationality. Union opposition may have slowed down the rate of retrenchment, but it is unlikely to be able to resist the logic of the rationalization process (Lang, 1998).

The impact of the ITP

The university produces graduates for the job market, research findings to support public policy, consultancy services for the government (including the parastatals) and the private sector (including NGOs), and, more generally, intellectual and advocacy services for groups in society and the nation.

Graduates

As mentioned above, until quite recently the public sector employed the majority of graduates. Manpower planning was designed to balance the output of secondary and higher education with the demand for senior government and parastatal staff. As recently as 1990, almost two-thirds of all formal employment was in these two sectors. With the coming

23

of economic liberalization, the privatization of parastatal corporations and the growth of the private economy, the demand for university graduates from UDSM and the rest of the higher education system has changed considerably. Freezing government recruitment and downsizing have resulted in graduate unemployment, though the extent and variation between disciplines are not known. The development of civil society organizations – trust funds, foundations, non-profit companies and NGOs – is another major force for change and source of employment. Financial flows from external sources, especially foreign aid and foreign direct investment (FDI), are also highly significant. Other important external forces relating to the rapid rise of information and communications technology are discussed below.

Are the number and quality of current graduates adequate to meet the demands of a rapidly changing job market? Is graduate unemployment on the increase? Are graduates going into self-employment and the informal sector? To answer these questions, the FOE (1985, 1989, 1995 and 1998) and Kaijage (2001) undertook tracer studies.

The FOE is unique in carrying out regular surveys tracking graduates into employment and assessing the quality and relevance of their studies and skills. The surveys are somewhat weakened by not following a common format and methodology over time and not reporting all important findings. Although the 1995 survey asked employers to rate the quality of FOE graduates according to criteria used in previous surveys, the results were not written up in the report (1995). Thus, it has not been possible to identify important trends over time, for example the extent to which private employers are satisfied with young graduates from the FOE.

The various studies reported virtually no unemployment among graduates, but it appears that it is taking longer for them to find work after graduation. Many graduates, especially the younger ones, expressed the desire to be self-employed. Fifty per cent, especially those working in the private sector, thought that self-employment was a good thing (FOE, 1995: 25). In the 1985 survey, only 27 per cent said they wanted to be self-employed (FOE, 1985: 77).

In 1985, over two-thirds (69 per cent) of employers rated FOE graduates' general technical ability as 'good', but only 22 per cent considered their specialized technical ability and 14 per cent their practical skills as good (FOE, 1998: 19). In 1989, the greatest gap between requirements and achievements was in practical skills (FOE, 1989: 56).

Box 3 reports some other important findings from the three studies.

The FCM study obtained data on 331 former students (about 17 per cent of 1981–96 graduates) and 77 employers. Eighty-three per cent of B. Com graduates in the sample had permanent employment and 12 per cent were unemployed. Nearly half the unemployed graduated in 1996. Of the employed B. Com graduates, 56 per cent worked for para-statals, 30 per cent for private companies and 14 per cent for the government. Of the 59 MBA holders sampled, 73 per cent worked for parastatals, 12 per cent for government, 10 per cent for private companies while 5 per cent were unemployed (Kaijage, 2000: 8, 11, 15).

The majority of B. Com graduates thought their studies did not 'prepare students to become self-employed after gradua-tion' (*ibid*.: Table 3.11).[2] A small majority of MBA graduates (53 per cent) said they wanted to be self-employed. According to both B. Com and MBA majors, entrepre-neurship and computer science were the main areas in which they would have benefited from 'deeper specialization' (*ibid*.: Table 3.14). These deficiencies are now being addressed with the introduction of an entrepreneurship course and the development of information and communica-tion technologies (ICT).

Box 3: Highlights from FOE tracer studies

Private sector grows...
84 per cent of graduates from 1977–80 period worked for the government and 16 per cent for the private sector. By 1992–4, the comparable figures were 64 per cent and 36 per cent.

Quality of studies falls ...
Three-quarters of 1977-80 graduates thought their educational background before entering FOE was 'fully adequate', compared with only 55 per cent of 1992–4 graduates. Half the 1977–80 graduates obtained first or upper second-class degrees, compared with 31 per cent in 1992–4.

Social selection increases ...
Nearly three-quarters (74 per cent) of 1977–80 graduates' fathers were illiterate or had only primary education, compared with 44 per cent of 1992–4 graduates' fathers. Fathers with secondary or higher education rose from 16 to 45 per cent during the same period. Regional selection remains high.

In the 1989 study, 29 per cent of students came from Kilimanjaro Region and a further 15 per cent from Kagera. For 1995, the comparable figures were 26 and 14 per cent respectively, indicating the continued domination of these two regions.

Dar is still the main source of employment ...
Over half (55 per cent) of graduates worked in Dar es Salaam in 1995, compared with 57 per cent in 1985.

Sources: FOE, 1989, 1995.

Research quality & relevance

The UDSM *Research Policy* (1998) 'maps the processes of identification of research needs and prioritization; research project identification and initiation; preparations and approval procedures for proposals, funding sources and modes; project control and monitoring; dissemination of research results and research effectiveness evaluation' (UDSM, 1998: vi).[3]

The newly established Directorate of Research and Publications (DRP) developed its own rolling strategic plan (1999/2000–2003/04), to implement the 1998 Research Policy. The plan includes producing a research policy and programme in all academic units; establishing databases for all publications; and publishing a prospectus, almanac, annual reports and a research bulletin. A major challenge for the DRP will be to improve the coordination and streamline the accounting requirements of the diverse agencies that fund research on the Hill.

How has research suffered as a result of the crisis of the 1980s described above? Do the research institutes and teaching departments at UDSM do quality research? How does the ITP address the question of improving research quality? Is the research being undertaken relevant to the development needs of the country? What influence have donors had on research? While not much is known about these issues, a few points are in order.

The academic audit (1998–9) was critical of the quality of teaching and research at UDSM.[4] Recurrent themes are the dependence on donor funding and the preference among staff for undertaking short-term consultancies rather than engaging in basic research. 'Research, particularly that conducted in the research institutes, has degenerated into consultancy services, with very little new knowledge being created in the process.' Consequently, 'all indications point to a sharp decline in quality journal articles' (UDSM, 1999a: 84).[5] The audit claims that dependence on external funding 'has affected research priorities' but gives no specifics on how or where this has happened.[6]

The academic audit also came to negative conclusions on the synergies between research and teaching. It appears that much more could be done to strengthen the linkages between

Box 4: Relevance of SIDA/SAREC support for research at UDSM [7]

The current phase of SIDA/SAREC support to UDSM coincided with the launch of the ITP, which SIDA/SAREC has actively supported to date. SIDA/SAREC considers that it has contributed 'to produce research results of relevance to development in Tanzania', citing the following examples: electric power distribution; the environmental consequences of gold mining and farming; coastal management; entrepreneurship; HIV/AIDS; and reproductive health. Other contributions include research capacity-building at UDSM and MUCHS, helping set up structures for research management (academic and financial) and building laboratories including the installation of scientific equipment (SIDA, 1999: 2). A 1996 external evaluation of SAREC support for AIDS research was extremely favourable. Research assisted the Tanzanian authorities in setting priorities for the National AIDS Control Programme and WHO in international surveillance, as well as improving laboratory diagnosis of HIV infection.

An independent evaluation of SIDA/SAREC support for environmental research in Tanzania (Alberts and Dougnac, 2000) found evidence of increased research capacity and curriculum improvements because of the projects (pp. 9-10). Research by the Department of Geology influenced the UNIDO/World Bank project on mitigating the environmental effects of small-scale gold mining (p. 14). More critical points include the level of research supervision fees (said to be too high) and the difficulties of having significant impact on policy processes generally.

the ITP and critical research undertaken by UDSM, particularly on the main campus.

Research can help advance the objectives of the ITP in a number of related ways. It can:

• help inform and orient national development strategy;
• help improve teaching;

- provide systematic evidence concerning the implementation of the ITP.

Box 4 provides some evidence on the first issue.

A recent evaluation of the Norwegian Council for Higher Education Programme for Development Research and Education (NUFU) research support for UDSM came to generally positive conclusions concerning the quality, if not the relevance, of Norwegian research support (Avenstrup and Swarts, 2000).

Evaluation of the ITP

The university Corporate Strategic Plan and the Five-Year Rolling Plan were drawn up by UDSM staff who underwent specific training for the exercise. This assured the requisite ownership of the planning process, which was done in-house through consultations and by trial and error. The process of preparing the three interrelated documents was a learning experience for the staff. The *Management Effectiveness Report* triggered the drawing up of the Corporate Strategic Plan, which in turn gave birth to the five-year rolling plans.

The lessons obtained from these experiences are reflected in the latest UDSM *Five-Year Rolling Strategic Plan for 1999/ 2000–2003/04* issued in September 1999. This is a much more elaborate, comprehensive and informative plan than the Corporate Strategic Plan adopted in 1994. It is underpinned by concrete measures based on an assessment of where the institution stood as of 1998–9, identifying the core strengths on which to capitalize and the weaknesses and threats to overcome.

In 1999, the university decided to evaluate the performance of the entire programme for the five years of its existence. The evaluation was done by a team of people outside the management circle of the university (Mgaya et al., 1999). The team used two sets of objectives as benchmarks for its evaluation. The first set derived from the corporate strategic plan itself. The second set was taken directly from the objectives of the five-year rolling plan. The evaluation was largely positive in its conclusions.

Notes

1   The Faculty of Law has used FOE lecture rooms for some years.
2   Those who expressed this view ranged from 63–72 per cent of 1979–85 graduates to 72 per cent of 1991–6 graduates.
3   The policy proposes an 8 per cent overhead for managing research projects, which seems low by international (and commercial) standards.
4   See Chapter 3 for a fuller discussion of the academic audit.
5   The Economic Research Bureau is singled out for particular criticism (Annex, pp. 88–90).
6   The audit comments that 'UDSM is not seen to be involved in ... major national programmes in health, education, energy, water and public administration' (UDSM, 1999a: 87).
7   See Appendix 3 for a fuller discussion of SIDA/SAREC research support to UDSM.

3 The Ingredients of Institutional Transformation

Financial strategies & sustainability

The University of Dar es Salaam has been in a state of chronic underfunding for many years. Even after the introduction of the ITP, the situation did not change much. However, through seminars organized by the ITP, people's attitude towards the whole question of funding has changed significantly. Table 2 summarizes the operating budget for the 1999–2000 academic year.

Table 2: Summary of income & expenditure for UDSM, 1999–2000

	TShm	US$m
Expenditure		
Recurrent	19,177	24.0
Development	7,112	8.9
Research	6,231	7.8
Transformation	1,855	2.3
Total	34,376	43.0
Income		
Student fees		
Government-sponsored	16,578	20.7
Privately-sponsored	1,209	1.5
UDSM internal generation	2,222	2.8
Government subsidy	2,213	2.8
Donor grants	8,283	10.4
Total	30,505	38.1
Financing gap	3,871	4.8

Source: UDSM, *Facts and Figures 1999/2000*, 1999.

External assistance

Most capital investment, postgraduate training and research are externally funded. Foreign financial and technical assistance has played a major role in the growth and development

31

of Tanzanian higher education and continues to figure as key in the ITP. The traditional *ad hoc* support to departments, institutes and faculties made the coordination of aid to UDSM virtually impossible. More recently, the Norwegian and Belgian governments have entered framework agreements with the university in recognition of this fact and as a means of supporting the ITP. Nevertheless, establishing a financial reporting system to track donor inputs has proved very difficult (UDSM, *Facts and Figures 1999/2000* 1999: 18–19). Donors tend to follow different budgeting and reporting systems and procedures and tend to reserve the right to control project finances. Similarly, deans, directors and principals often fail to report aid income and expenditure to the administration on time. Moves are afoot to tighten up reporting requirements for both donors and recipients (UDSM, 1999b: 20).

Major donors to UDSM include SIDA/SAREC (research), NORAD (expansion of facilities), DANIDA (research), the Netherlands (entrepreneurship and other areas) and GTZ

Table 3: Major donor support to UDSM, 1996–2002

Donor	Main activities	US$m	Time frame
NORAD/NUFU	Construction	11.1	1997–2001
SIDA/SAREC	Research	5.7	1997–2000
Netherlands	Various	5.0	1996–2002
DANIDA	Research	4.7	1996–8
Belgium	Various	2.8	1997–2000
IDRC	Research	1.4	1996–2001
GTZ–Germany	Engineering	0.8	1995–8
Ireland	Engineering	0.8	1996–8
Other[a]	Various	2.0	1996–2001
Total		34.3	

Note: a) USA, British Council, Governments of Finland and Switzerland, World Health Organization, Ford and MacArthur Foundations.
Source: UDSM, *Facts and Figures 1999/2000*: 91–3.

(Faculty of Engineering). Table 3 summarizes major donor aid activities.

It is difficult to calculate with any precision the proportion of aid in total university budgets. Aid accounts for most of the development budget, but for how much of recurrent costs? Is the trend towards more or less dependence on donors? One source suggests that almost half of UDSM resources came from donors in the early to mid-1990s. The highest degree of dependence was in engineering and science, followed by arts and social sciences, commerce and management, education and law (Wield, 1995: 35). In 1991–2, nearly two-thirds of total donor support went to the engineering and science faculties (*ibid.*: 37).

There were an estimated 133 separate linking arrangements between higher education institutions elsewhere and UDSM faculties, departments and institutes, with arts and social sciences leading (30), followed by MUCHS (22), engineering and science (20 each), and IDS (10) (*ibid.*)[1]

The extent of departmental-level donor support and the availability of individual consultancy opportunities – whereby professors can earn the equivalent of their monthly salaries from a few days' work – weaken this commitment to the ITP. Aid money may help entrench vested interests that prevent desirable organizational changes, including the merging of research and teaching departments and institutes. Wield concludes that 'The overall impression of donor support to UDSM is how important it has become, and how relatively weak it is as institutional support' (1995: 42). The management's awareness of the pitfalls of uncoordinated support has led to the introduction of framework agreements between agencies and the university rather than with individual departments or institutes. However, individual frame agreements still need to be coordinated.

Table 4 summarizes estimates of external funding needs for the period 2000–05.

Table 4: Summary of UDSM external funding needs, 2000–05

Priority support areas	US$m
Improved teaching and learning	13.2
Research and publications	4.7
Organizational culture and management	5.8
Infrastructure	36.5
Staff development	5.4
Total	65.6

Source: UDSM, *Facts and Figures 1999/2000.*

The ITP has attracted substantial donor interest and investment. Future donor support needs to be better coordinated and increasingly based on performance. There is no reason why donors should not continue to support the ITP in the various ways mentioned above, provided coordination and efficiency improve.

Fee-paying students

Previously, members of staff saw the problem of funding as a government problem. There was marked resistance to introducing fee-paying students and market-oriented programmes. The mood has now changed because of the university's decision to allow the faculties and departments to use the revenue accruing from these sources to improve the teaching-learning process within their own units. In the case of consultancy, the bulk of the revenue goes to the individual and only a part to the faculty or department. A number of faculties and departments have been able to acquire computers, furnish their offices and even fix air conditioners with the income they generated. The decisive factor here is that they have been authorized to use the income generated.

Commercializing service units

In response to dwindling government funding and as a cost-cutting measure, the university within the ITP retrenched in 1996 about 700 support and administrative staff and commercialized one of the cafeterias, the Silversands Hotel and the Dar es Salaam University Press (transforming it into a limited liability company).

It has also begun to tap income-generating activities and consultancy as new sources of income.

Income Generation Unit

In February 1998, the university established the Income Generation Unit (IGU). Its function is to promote and co-ordinate income-generating activities for the university, mainly by attracting third parties for the commercial management of university assets (including land, office accommodation, hostels, conference, catering and secretarial services). To date, only a relatively small proportion of the potential sources of income have been exploited,[2] though others (halls of residence, cafeteria and canteens, cleaning and gardening services) were due to be (Chungu, 2000).

University Consultancy Bureau (UCB)

Although most faculties have policies in place, attempts to tax consultancies through institutional overheads have proved unpopular among the university staff.[3] The university has approved a consultancy policy, but there are no clear criteria for costing overheads in individual faculties, and the degree of reporting of consultancies to the university administration is not known. The FOE has been more successful than the University Consultancy Bureau (UCB) in formalizing and charging overheads for individual consultancy work.[4] In general, donors do not have a policy on working through departments or institutes rather than individual consultants, thus complicating efforts to standardize outside work

35

performed by the academic workforce.

In 1990, the Faculty of Engineering established the Bureau for Industrial Cooperation (BICO), whose function was to transfer technology from the university to local industry through consultancy and training activities. In 1996–7 alone, BICO realized a gross income of US$430,000. Encouraged by the success of the FOE initiative, in 1993–4 the university decided to launch a consultancy bureau whose main function would be to promote and coordinate consultancy activities university-wide. But the UCB does not appear to be functioning optimally, for a number of reasons:

- it lacks a strong institutional base (as compared with BICO);
- it faces stiff competition, especially in social science-based consultancies;
- most university staff are unfamiliar with or lack consultancy tendering skills;
- many UDSM staff do not report their consultancy work to the UCB.

The consequences of consultancies not being reported to the university include:

- the university does not receive its entitled overheads although university time and facilities are often used;
- the university is not able to exert quality control over the work undertaken;
- the academic staff member is not able to use the consultancy output for job promotion;
- consultancy work may reduce the time spent on teaching and course preparation, to the detriment of students.

Consultancy has an important role to play in the life of the university as a way of learning by doing and enhancing the linkage between theory and practice. It helps to stimulate and foster entrepreneurial attitudes. It is, however, important to make sure that consultancy work is not carried out at the expense of teaching and research.

Unit costs

The university is trying to persuade the government to pay fees for the students it sponsors, in place of the present practice of giving a lump sum grant to the university, which does not take account of the actual needs of the university or the number of students enrolled. The indications are that the government is willing to consider this option, provided the unit cost computation is reasonable and is based on acceptable efficiency norms.

Response to market forces

The university has attempted to respond to market forces in two ways. Firstly, it has introduced courses designed to encourage students to become job creators or self-employed upon graduation and has established an entrepreneurship centre for this purpose under the coordination of the Faculty of Commerce and Management (FCM). The Faculty of Engineering has introduced an optional course in 'techno-entrepreneurship' for its finalists.

The university has also tried to encourage faculties, colleges and departments to carry out tracer studies and market surveys in order to update their curricula based on the results. The main constraint is the cost of such studies (see Chapter 5).

Arguably, the most difficult challenge facing the university with regard to this issue is how to change the students' mindset from the public-sector mentality of dependency and wastefulness to the private-sector mentality of entrepreneurship, frugality and value for money. Unless this transformation takes place, there is little hope that the university's products will fit the new socio-economic environment which is emerging in Tanzania today. This issue requires study.

Restructuring of the curriculum & the academic environment

One of the most remarkable undertakings of the ITP was the conducting of an academic audit in 1998–9. The audit panel consisted of six academics, three of whom were external to UDSM and three internal. Their report is a frank and open assessment of the institutional strengths and weaknesses of UDSM, and provides extremely useful information not only for understanding but also for identifying areas for external support. One of the strengths highlighted by the report is the fact that 68 per cent of UDSM academic staff have doctorates. The report, however, is highly critical of the state of the curriculum review. Of the 63 departments surveyed, only 15 (24 per cent) had reviewed their curricula in the previous five years. Of the remaining 48 departments, nine (14 per cent) had reviewed their curricula within the last 5–10 years. The remaining 39 (62 per cent of the total) had not conducted a review of their curricula for a period of more than 25 years or since their establishment.

This means that for the majority of departments there is no formal process of integrating new knowledge generated through research into the teaching and learning process. The report is also critical of the rigid nature of the academic programmes that to some extent gives rise to duplication and fragmentation. It encourages rationalizing programmes to enhance efficiency through reclustering. It also urges a review of curricula in response to current labour market requirements and the adoption of the semester system to replace the existing term system.

The conclusions and recommendations of the academic audit have been included in the *Rolling Strategic Plan* (UDSM,

1999: 81–9). Some units have already taken steps to merge and review their activities accordingly. The Faculty of Commerce and Management has reviewed its curricula and adopted a semester model. It has also introduced demand-driven courses, such as an evening course leading to the B.B.A. The Department of Mathematics has also introduced a demand-driven course.

Staff development

University policy requires academic members of staff to have a doctorate or to strive to obtain one as soon as possible. However, the university does not have adequate resources to help staff observe this policy, and individual staff are left largely on their own trying to observe it. The process is made easier when the link programmes include a training component. Nevertheless, even here the going is difficult because many link programmes give only partial support for doctorate training. The preferred arrangement is the cost-reducing 'sandwich' model, in which the candidate registers at the home institution but is given time to spend at a foreign institution for doing extensive reading, experimentation and/or analysis under its supervision on terms mutually agreed by the institutions involved. Projects funded by NUFU, SIDA/SAREC and VLIR (Vlaamse Interuniversitaire Raad) provide for this kind of sandwich training. Other advantages of this arrangement are that:

- it promotes closer institutional cooperation through joint supervision of the candidate;
- it enables candidates to maintain close contact with the home institution and tailor their research to local needs;
- it provides candidates with a ready-made research agenda for post-doctoral research;
- it gives candidates – particularly those who have done their first and second degrees locally – international exposure.

39

USHEPIA has also adopted this model of training, and members of the UDSM academic community are benefiting from it. A possible disadvantage of the arrangement is that candidates could take much longer to complete their studies if there is no proper institutional coordination. Dar es Salaam's sandwich programme with the University of Lund (Sweden) in the 1970s and 1980s suffered from this difficulty.

ICT policies & implementation

This section focuses on the following areas:[5]

- strategic planning
- utilization of ICT in faculties and departments
- the library
- the African Virtual University
- management information systems.

ICT strategic planning & implementation: the Computing Centre

As part of the ITP and with assistance from Delft (Netherlands) University of Technology,[6] UDSM approved an ICT Policy Plan and an ICT Master Plan in 1995. The University Computing Centre was given the role of overseeing ICT implementation and of serving as an IT resource-management centre for the entire university.

The university has approved the transformation of the Computing Centre into a limited liability company, with the university owning all the shares in the first instance (Mutagahywa and Bakari, 2000: 6). It is intended as a means of generating off-campus income to help sustain ICT services at UDSM.[7]

Campus backbone & access to computers

The campus computer network backbone has been put in

Box 5: Computing Centre

'At the University of Dar es Salaam we have realized that the on-going information revolution has, and will, continue changing the way we teach and learn, the way we do research and above all, the way we provide our services to the community at large. Hence the University of Dar es Salaam has evolved a vision of becoming a leading centre of excellence in ICT, providing world-class services to students, staff and the wider community outside the University'.

Briefing on ICT by Vice-Chancellor Luhanga for President Mpaka at the inauguration of the UDSM Computing Centre, 28 September 1999.

---

place; all 26 academic buildings, the Computing Centre and the library are interconnected. As a start, each building has at least one point connected to the backbone.

Eight kilometres of high-speed fibre-optic cable were laid to make the backbone possible. Its current transmission speed is 10 Mbps, which will increase to 100 Mbps when upgrading activities are completed. MUCHS and the University College of Lands and Architectural Studies (UCLAS) are linked to the backbone through a 2-Mbps wireless connection and fibre-optic links are planned with the main campus. In addition, the Computing Centre will soon begin experimenting with a wireless link from Zanzibar to the mainland to connect the Institute of Maritime Studies to the campus backbone.

All departments on the three campuses have Local Area Networks (LANs).[8] The main campus and the two college campuses have fibre-optic backbone networks connecting all buildings. The UCLAS campus is linked to the main campus by an optical fibre link while the college of Health Sciences is linked by an 11-Mbps wireless link. The student halls of residence on the main campus are also linked to the

41

backbone network by fibre-optic cable. Students' access to network resources is provided through pools of computers (Public Access Rooms) built in facilities and student halls of residence.

A large percentage of the teaching staff have easy access to computers through project funds. Postgraduate students, particularly those in the faculties of Engineering and Sciences, also have reasonable access, although this is not the case in every department. Undergraduates are the ones who experience the most difficulty in getting computer time. The university estimates that it should have one computer for every ten undergraduate students, with more PCs for those studying for postgraduate degrees. As part of the university's ICT upgrading activities, plans are under way to put computer labs in each faculty. As a start, the faculties will receive 20 PCs each (somewhat fewer in the smaller faculties). The computer labs will be fully networked and have access to the campus backbone and the internet.

Internet connectivity

When the university's Very Small Aperture Terminal (VSAT) was first installed, its link was to South Africa at a speed of 64 Kbps. The speed was upgraded to 128 Kbps in 1998, with a direct link to the United States, and to 512 Kbps in 2000, with SIDA/SAREC support. Further upgrading to 1 Mbps is planned.

Cost recovery

Faculties and departments pay US$50 a month for each computer hooked up to the internet through the campus backbone. This charge covers unlimited internet access. The Computing Centre hopes to reduce the fee to US$5 a month with the faculty-wide LANs. UDSM proposes to charge students a highly subsidized rate of US$1.00 per month, which will include 20 hours a month of internet access.

The university is also allowed to act as an Internet Service Provider for other academic institutions and NGOs. Other academic institutions in Dar es Salaam, such as the Open University of Tanzania (OUT), pay US$200 a month for a wireless connection to UDSM.

The Computing Centre maintains the UDSM home page, which can be found at http://www.udsm.ac.tz. While the web site as a whole is due to be redesigned, some faculties are only now preparing their initial input.[9] Even so, the UDSM site contains valuable information, including information about the university, degree and academic programmes, admission requirements and administration.[10]

As an example of what a good website can offer, the Faculty of Science home page, maintained by the Chemistry Department, is particularly interesting. Not only is there information about degrees and the department on the site, but there are also tables of contents from the *Tanzania Journal of Science* dating from 1990.[11] The home page of the Natural Products Research Network for Eastern and Central Africa (NAPRECA) is also hosted by the Department of Chemistry.

Utilization of ICT in faculties & departments

Students (and also staff in some areas) are highly limited in their access to ICT facilities. In the faculties of Law and Education, several postgraduate students said that they had no access at all to ICT facilities, and most of them are not computer-literate. In this context, the Faculty of Engineering should be commended for introducing a faculty-wide computer literacy course in the first year of the undergraduate programme and an optional course at the postgraduate level.

Arts & Social Sciences

One-third of all UDSM students study for degrees in one of the nine departments at FASS. ICT utilization was slow to develop here until 1997, when FASS began a strategic planning process and incorporated ICT into its planning. Before then, a few departments, notably Economics (including the Economic Research Bureau) and Political Science, had computers on an ad hoc basis, but there was no faculty-wide approach to their acquisition or utilization.

FASS came to a realization of the need for computers fairly late, holding to the view that the subjects it taught did not require computer skills. By the time the faculty realized what it was missing, several large grants to the university were in mid-cycle, and the donor pie was already fully divided.

Even though the faculty has not yet received large amounts of funding earmarked for ICT, strategic planning has had important positive effects. First of all, departments are working together. For example, the Ford Foundation provided two separate grants to the faculty – one to Political Science and one to the East Africa Uongozi Institute (a regional summer school for undergraduates housed at the faculty), which included funds to acquire computers. Staff decided to pool the computers and create a computer lab, for a total of 20 PCs. In addition, FASS as a whole made a decision to use a portion of its support from the university to acquire computers – 40 in all. To do this, the faculty had to forgo other purchases, but computers were considered more important. Thirty-four of these computers were placed in the computer lab; four will go to departments sorely in need of them. Plans are under way to acquire more computers and to create a special room for postgraduate students.

The lab will be at the disposal of the entire faculty and will be used for course work. In addition to Microsoft Office Suite, the computers are loaded with two programming languages (C++ and Pascal). The Computing Centre advised the faculty on the computer specifications. In addition to this large computer lab, the departments still have their own special computer rooms. Geography, for example, needs dedicated computers for GIS and other software; Political Science has placed at least one computer in every classroom. Economics is one of the best-equipped departments. Not every department is equally fortunate in terms of either numbers of computers or computer capacity. Much of the equipment dates from pre-1997 days when not everyone understood the importance of ICT. The faculty now needs to take stock of individual departmental needs and the needs of the faculty as a whole. Planning is already in place, but an ICT audit could be undertaken to determine how many computers are needed, where they should be placed and what kind of software is necessary.

While FASS has moved forward on ICT implementation, it is hard to say whether the students are utilizing ICT efficiently to access information. Up to now, online internet searches would have been difficult. and the faculty estimates that only about 40 per cent of the students routinely carry out CD-ROM searches for their research projects. The addition of an information retrieval skills module to the social science research methods course, which is required at both under-graduate and graduate levels, would help to sharpen students' abilities in this area.

Engineering

The Faculty of Engineering is widely considered a leader in ICT at UDSM. The faculty has instituted a compulsory information technology course for first-year undergraduate students, something that other faculties are only now beginning to do.[12]

The problem is that there are not enough computers for undergraduates to use regularly once they finish this course and have learned the rudiments of information technology. This is true of all four departments in the faculty, including Electrical Engineering and Chemical and Process Engineering. Since the postgraduate student population is smaller, it is easier

45

to accommodate their needs than those of undergraduates, and their coursework demands computer access.[13] Many of the teaching staff have computers, but they are not necessarily owned by the departments to which they are attached.

Both the Electrical Engineering and Chemical and Process Engineering Departments have installed their own LANs. In addition, the dean's office is partially networked. All ICT-related work is handled within the faculty – from wiring and maintaining the LAN to creation of the faculty home page.

Engineering students are encouraged to carry out CD-ROM searches in the library before submitting research proposals. In fact, the Department of Chemical and Process Engineering requires a CD-ROM search from its students.[14] Several lecturers estimated that the availability of scientific literature databases on CD-ROM has reduced the time needed for a PhD dissertation literature review from 18 months to 6–8 months. Increasingly faculty members are using the internet to do online searches of current literature.

Sciences

In general, the Faculty of Sciences is well equipped with computers. Every staff member in Chemistry and Mathematics has a computer (desktop or laptop). In Geology, about 60 per cent of staff have personal computers. Chemistry, Mathematics and part of Geology are fully networked to the campus backbone. The situation vis-à-vis students is not so good. Undergraduate students, particularly in Biology, experience considerable difficulty in obtaining access to computers. There are 500 undergraduate students in Biology and only ten computers for them to use, despite the university's desired ratio of one computer for every ten students. Although the situation is a little better for postgraduate students, they still do not have easy access.

Teaching staff and students are accessing online information resources. With project support, the faculty subscribes to

Current Contents online for physical and life sciences, but continuing subscription to this journal is not assured. In the Chemistry Department, users also consult table of contents and other information on *ChemWeb*. Students are also familiar with *Science Citation Index* on CD-ROM, which is housed in the library.[15] Postgraduate science students also benefit from CD-ROM databases and internet access to reduce the time needed for their literature reviews.

ICT for teaching & learning

The university is now embarking on two activities that it hopes will change the way teaching and learning take place at UDSM. The first, funded by Belgium, is called the Technology Enhanced Independent Learning (TEIL) Project. The aim is to create a virtual learning environment for both students and faculty. Three faculties submitted proposals to receive TEIL funds—Commerce, Engineering and Law. After considering these proposals, the selection committee chose the Faculty of Law (FOL) for the first phase of the project. The second initiative involves the creation of a Centre for Continuing Education, which is not yet funded, but is under discussion with the Netherlands as part of their ongoing support for ICT implementation at the university.

The Computing Centre hopes to play a role in these initiatives by creating a user-friendly environment for teaching and learning on the network. A five-member development team is in place; three of them are now in the United States evaluating different software packages that can be used for this purpose.

The UDSM Library

UDSM library functions are manifold – everything from responsibility for the master's degree programme in information sciences to expanding floor space to accommodate more users and providing reader services. This discussion concentrates on

---

Box 6: The Library

'The fundamental role of the UDSM Main Library is to provide adequate and relevant information resources to support quality teaching, research and consultancy services. Both the academic staff and students depend heavily on the Main Library for information that is necessary in pursuing their programmes. Thus, the university considers the Main Library a very central organ in the teaching and learning process at the University.'

Source: UDSM, *Five-Year Rolling Strategic Plan 1999–2000–2003/2004*. detailed version, No. 3, 1999.

---

automation, using ICT for information access (CD-ROM and internet, including e-mail) and journals (subscriptions and document delivery). The latter is very important, for it does no good to learn about relevant articles if they are not attainable.

Automation
In late 1998, with funding from the Netherlands and Sweden (SIDA/SAREC), the library began implementing the Library Information System (LIBIS) project. The Netherlands also provides technical assistance to implement the system. The goal of LIBIS is to automate all library activities – including the library catalogue, loans, acquisitions and serials. Eventually, LIBIS will be available on the library LAN, on the campus backbone and via the internet. Users everywhere will be able to access information on UDSM library holdings. In addition to the main library, the plans call for incorporating faculty/departmental libraries and the libraries of MUCHS and UCLAS. It is an enormous undertaking.

The library installed the automation software, ADLIB, in November 1998. The vendor trained two library staff members in the Netherlands in its use. In addition, further training was organized at UDSM for more staff.

To date, 10,000 records have been entered – about 1 per cent of the total. The library has been hampered by a shortage of computers. Only eight PCs are available for data entry, and only one of them is dedicated to the LIBIS project. The library has placed an order for 25 computers, ten of which will be reserved for data entry. The pace of data entry is expected to accelerate with the arrival of more computers and during vacation periods.

CD-ROM

CD-ROM services in the UDSM Library began in 1992, with a grant from the Carnegie Corporation of New York. In 1994, UDSM participated in a three-year CD-ROM Pilot Project of the American Association for the Advancement of Science, whereby seven African universities were provided with seven bibliographic CD-ROM databases and document delivery. The goal was to evaluate how well CD-ROM and document delivery could supplement and even replace journal subscriptions when necessary (see Abegaz and Levey, 1996 for a full report).

The library has four computer terminals dedicated to CD-ROM searching and is expecting a CD-ROM server, which will make it possible to conduct a CD-ROM search from any computer on the library LAN via the campus backbone.

As UDSM improves its campus backbone and internet capacity and increases the number of computers available to students, the library could consider subscribing to some of these databases online rather than in CD-ROM form. The online version of *Science Citation Index*, for example, includes access to the ISI document delivery service and back years of data to 1973, seven more years than the CD-ROM edition.

There are no accurate statistics on CD-ROM utilization at the library because it has decided to forgo monitoring in favour of providing services, which is understandable. According to the university librarian:

In real terms, the number of users has gone up. Due to shortage of staff and the fact that some of the CD-ROM users can use them on their own, we decided to pay more attention to helping with Internet searches and to the LIBIS project. Thus, recording of statistics are indicative rather than actual figures because recording is done by users on a voluntary basis...Chances of people forgetting or ignoring to record are very high.[16]

Although the numbers are only indicative, almost all of the recorded users are students (878 out of 1,018). Few of the teaching staff appear to use the CD-ROM databases in the library. If this is the case, the question arises as to how teaching staff keep up with recent developments in their respective disciplines and conduct literature reviews in preparation for their own research projects.

The library has been able to maintain its CD-ROM services since the conclusion of the CD-ROM pilot project at the end of 1996. It has cancelled some CD-ROM subscriptions, added others and presently subscribes to 18 databases. According to the library's figures, in 1998–9 the five most popular databases were: *Sociofile*; *Compendix Plus*; *Life Sciences Collection*; *GeoBase*; and *Science Citation Index*.

The library may need to work with users to help them understand different kinds of information resources. Even if teaching staff and some students use the internet for their literature reviews, they should also appreciate the significance of the bibliographic databases to which the library subscribes. It is difficult to carry out a retrospective literature review without them. The only substitute for the CD-ROM edition of *Science Citation Index* is the online version. Both require subscriptions, however.

Journal subscriptions & document delivery
The library subscribes to about 550 journals. SIDA/SAREC pays for some 300, a few are donations and the remaining titles are purchased with library funds. The library has not

been accessing online journals that require subscription.

For the most part, the library uses the British Library Document Supply Centre for document delivery requests. Document delivery is free for UDSM students and staff; non-university library users pay for the cost of the document ordered.

E-mail & internet

Because student access to computers is still very limited on the UDSM campus, the library has been providing an invaluable e-mail service at a charge of TSh100 (US$0.14) per message. In 1999, the library recorded 239,350 outgoing and 272,325 incoming messages!

Internet use costs TSh300 (US$0.43) for 15 minutes of online time. It is not widely used, and very few people come to the library to use internet for research purposes. They primarily log on to free e-mail services.

African Virtual University

The pilot phase of the African Virtual University (AVU) node at the UDSM began in July 1997 and ended in June 1999. During this period, the University Computing Centre co-ordinated the AVU project. The AVU provided UDSM with a receive-only satellite dish, downloading equipment (decoders and accessories), a fax machine, two television screens and 25 used computers (Dell 486s). In early 1999, the AVU at UDSM was transferred to the Income Generation Unit, and a full-time coordinator was hired.

To date, the AVU has offered a limited number of short courses, but inadequate equipment has hampered their effectiveness. Since the satellite dish is receive-only, inter-activity takes place through e-mail, telephone and fax. The computers have very limited capacity in terms of both speed and hard disk space. In addition, because of power problems in the room where the computers are located, only four PCs are fully operational and linked to the campus backbone.

51

This situation may change in the near future, however. The AVU is gearing up to offer undergraduate degree courses in computer science, electrical engineering and computer engineering. Not every AVU node will offer these courses, but UDSM expects to be one of the AVU degree pioneers. It will require careful planning because the Faculty of Engineering is already running degree programmes in computer science and electrical engineering and plans to begin a computer engineering degree programme soon. UDSM believes that the demand is sufficiently high to accommodate both the UDSM and AVU engineering degrees. Moreover, both the AVU and the Faculty of Engineering will benefit from the introduction of these courses; UDSM will provide teaching staff and some of the AVU modules will be relevant to UDSM curricula. The FOE plans to purchase these modules from the AVU.

Terms of reference will be needed for the AVU degree courses. The plan is for the AVU to set up as a private university with its own degree programmes, but hosted by the University of Dar es Salaam. In addition, the AVU will have to improve its technical infrastructure. It will need more and better computers, a full LAN and more bandwidth. It is unclear whether the World Bank, the sponsor of the AVU, or UDSM will have to bear the costs of the necessary upgrading.

Automation of UDSM management information

With funding from bilateral Dutch and German sources, the university has two automation projects under way – the Financial Information Systems (FIS) Project and the Academic Registrar Information System (ARIS) Project (see Luhanga, 1999: 3–4).

FIS is in its final stages of implementation. The physical infrastructure and hardware are in place as are the accounting and payroll systems databases. The payroll system is fully operational at university level, and the computerization of accounting records is at a very advanced stage. Using the campus backbone, the system will soon extend to the faculties. In addition, this project has made it possible to set up an External Funds Administration (EFA) unit to assist UDSM in computerizing records of the funds it receives from external sources. The goal of ARIS is help the university create a computerized information system for academic administration processes – including admissions, student records and grading. The project got under way in 2000.

In addition to these university-wide efforts, the FOE is creating its own administrative systems for staff data and student records. UDSM faculty members are doing the work to set it up.

Notes

1   MUCHS was formerly Muhimbili University College.
2   The university's magnificent 45-metre swimming pool, financed by the Aga Khan in the 1960s, is the largest in the country. Unused for many years, a Norwegian grant recently paid for its rehabilitation. Although entry fees are charged, there are currently no plans to privatize the pool's management.
3   The Institute of Resource Assessment, for example, takes 40 per cent of staff consultancy fees as institutional overheads.
4   From late 1996 to February 1998, 20 consultancies were channelled through the UCB, generating TSh72 million (US$90,000).
5   In preparing this section, time did not permit a visit to each faculty; nor was an up-to-date university-wide audit of the computers on campus easily available. Visits were made to the Faculties of Engineering and of Arts and Social Sciences. The former is well advanced in ICT, while the latter is eagerly trying to make up for lost time. In addition, interviews were held with Prof. M.H.H. Nkunya, Chief Academic Officer and former Dean of the Faculty of Science, and Dr C.C. Joseph of the Chemistry department, focusing on their perception of ICT implementation in sciences.
6   Funding to support this project comes from the Netherlands Ministry for International Cooperation. Under Netherlands funding promoting

South–South cooperation, Eduardo Mondlane University in Mozambique has sent experts to UDSM to help the computer centre instal its VSAT satellite system.

7   For instance, the 512K VSAT Internet connection costs the University US$8,250 per month, almost double what it paid for the 128K connection.

8   Faculty of Engineering (Electrical Engineering, Chemical Processing and part of the Dean's office), the Department of Chemistry, part of the Faculty of Education and the main administration building were the first to create their own ad hoc LANs.

9   Although it may seem of peripheral relevance, websites are important. They are an indication of the importance a university places on ICT, and they can be a vehicle for transmitting information to students and teaching staff (syllabi, bibliographies, course notes, etc). Equally important, they are the university's face to the outside world.

10   UDSM is also responsible for the Tanzanian website domain registration of academic and governmental institutions.

11   Abstracts were added in 1998.

12   The Faculty of Law undergraduate IT course was scheduled to begin in the 2000–01 academic year. Some faculty members estimate that fewer than 5 per cent of the students are computer-literate.

13   There are approximately 1,000 undergraduates and 200 postgraduates in the Faculty of Engineering – the largest concentration of postgraduates of any faculty in the university.

14   The University Library subscribes to *Compendix Plus* on CD-ROM, probably the best broadbased engineering-sciences database on the market. It includes bibliographic citations and abstracts of a broad range of journals, conference proceedings, reports and books.

15   Access to *Chemical Abstracts Services* (CAS) is beyond the means of the department, however.

16   E-mail communication from Julita Nawe, university librarian, 4 March 2000.

4 Economic, Political & Educational Sector Transformations

Recent political & economic trends

Along with the rest of sub-Saharan Africa, Tanzania is experiencing a period of rapid political and economic change. Heavily influenced by the international financial institutions (IFIs) and bilateral donors, the process of change encompasses both political pluralism and economic liberalization. Tanzania's starting point for these basic transitions was a highly centralized, single-party state, weak civil society institutions and an economy largely dominated by state-owned industrial, financial and marketing monopolies.

The likelihood of a successful transformation process at UDSM is conditioned by the nature and magnitude of these changes. For example, trends towards more representative government will affect the extent to which the political elite is prepared to relax central government control of the finance and management of higher education. Similarly, economic growth affects the country's tax base and the possibility of increasing official funding for higher education as well as the potential for cost-sharing measures. Economic growth is a precondition for job creation and the employment (including self-employment) of UDSM and other graduates. Finally, policy choices (and non-choices) influence the total revenues available for education overall and higher education in particular, as well as the nature and extent of measures taken to reduce recruitment inequalities based on class, gender, or other factors.

Educational and employment policies have had to adjust to reflect these emerging political and economic trends. Yet the reality of continued low enrolments and poor quality and performance bear testament to how much still remains to be done.

Appendix 5 provides an overview of these trends and policies, which are summarized below.[1]

A partial transition to democracy

Tanzania held multi-party elections in October 1995. The ruling Chama Cha Mapinduzi (CCM) party returned to power

55

with a comfortable majority of seats in the National Assembly. Factionalism and personality conflicts weakened the major opposition parties, which did not mount a serious challenge to CCM in the October 2000 elections.

According to one group of observers, the major obstacles to democratization include the reluctance of the old political class to loosen its grip on power; systematic corruption; weak performance and poor capacities of the opposition parties; inadequate civil-society capacity and resources; lack of resources and quality staff in the independent media; poor facilities and resources in the judiciary; a general culture of accepting an authoritarian, hierarchical social structure; and lack of public information and knowledge of rights (Peter et al., 1995).[2]

Corruption has been a major policy issue since 1994, when President Mkapa declared that fighting corruption would be a key concern of his presidency. However, many feel that top officials do not support the President's anti-corruption strategy.

A partial transition to a market economy

The profound economic crisis of the late 1970s and early 1980s led to the reluctant adoption of a World Bank-IMF structural adjustment programme and the gradual abandonment of the command economy after 1985. Policies encouraging foreign investment have had some success, particularly in gold mining, which is likely to be a major foreign-exchange earner in years to come.

After years of economic stagnation, GNP growth has picked up in recent years, although it is still well below the level required to make a significant dent in current poverty levels. Agricultural export performance has varied between sectors. The government's strict fiscal policy has virtually eliminated budget deficits and inflation has fallen from an average of over 30 per cent in the 1980s to single digits in the year 2000 (URT, Bank of Tanzania, 1999).

Foreign aid finances about one-third of the recurrent budget and almost all public investment. Structural adjustment borrowing from the IFIs after 1985 resulted in the escalation of external debt from US$1.5 billion in 1982 to nearly US$9 billion in December 1998 (Embassy of Sweden, 1995). Tanzania has qualified for debt relief under the revised Heavily Indebted Poor Country Initiative (HIPC2) whereby debt relief is conditional on enhanced anti-poverty programmes. Though significant, current growth rates are insufficient to have a major impact on the incidence of poverty.[3]

In summary, major opportunities in the present policy regime include good financial discipline and a sustainable inflation rate, positive growth in GDP, improvements in tax collection, important revenue prospects from mineral investments, reduced debt burden under HIPC2, continued donor confidence and continued political stability. But there are also serious constraints: the poor quality of social services; low levels of government transparency and accountability; continued pervasive poverty and youth unemployment; and depressed prices for agricultural exports.

Trends in primary & secondary education[4]

Net primary school enrolment rates were 57 per cent in 1998 compared with 67 per cent a decade earlier (TADREG, 1998). Only one-third of seven-to-nine-year-olds are in school, rising to over 80 per cent of 10–14-year-olds (URT, MOES and MSTHE, 1997: 3).

Secondary enrolments grew by more than half (56 per cent) between 1990 and 1998, with all the increase taking place in the state sector. Private-school enrolments actually fell during this period. Despite recent growth, secondary enrolment rates in Tanzania are still among the lowest in Africa and the world. Table 5 summarizes the recent trends.

Urban–rural and district-level inequalities in primary educational inputs and outputs are significant, despite official

57

Table 5: Trends in primary & secondary school enrolment, 1990–98 (numbers & percentages of students)

	1990	1992	1994	1996	1998
Primary	3,379,000	3,599,580	3,793,201	3,937,204	4,035,209
Primary net enrolment rate (%)	54.2	54.2	55.2	56.3	57.0
Secondary	145,242	175,776	186,246	199,093	226,903
Private enrolment rate (%)	57.4	55.2	55.2	51.1	45.2

Sources: Penrose (1997); URT, MSTHE (2000).

policies aimed at equity. On a combined index based on enrolment rates, proportion of Grade A teachers, pupil-teacher ratios, class size and school-leaving examination results, eight of the top ten districts were regional headquarters (TADREG, 1998: Table 4).

Gender inequalities in schooling increase from the primary level upwards. Girls' performance is significantly below that of boys at the primary school leaving examination, particularly in mathematics, as well as at 'O' level (Form 4) and 'A' levels (Form 6) (TADREG, 1990). There is some evidence that social inequalities in school selection have increased over time (Malekela, 1983; Cooksey et al., 1991).

The growth of private secondary schooling in the 1980s led to growing inequalities in educational opportunities (URT, MOEC, 1999b). By 1992, Christian churches ran nearly half of the private secondary schools whereas only 6 per cent were run by the official Muslim school body (Cooksey et al., 1994: 225).

Trends in employment

Economic liberalization in the last 15 years or so has led to the rapid informalization of the urban and rural economy. It is estimated that the informal sector accounts for 60 per cent of non-agricultural employment. Value added in informal

58

manufacturing, commerce and personal services exceeds that generated in the formal sector (Dar, 1995).

The monthly wage of a male graduate in 1995 was three times that of an uneducated male; for females, the ratio was nine times greater. Male secondary-school leavers and graduates earned TSh7,763 (US$9.70) and TSh12,048 (US$15.06) a month, respectively, while for women average monthly earnings were TSh7,390 (US$9.24) and TSh18,141 (US$22.68) (*ibid.*).[5]

The Labour Force Survey found that 42 per cent of formal-sector workers were in the civil service, 23 per cent in parastatal companies and 35 per cent in the private sector. The retrenchment of civil servants, the privatization and closure of parastatals and the (perhaps) growing investment in the private sector will probably lead to a rapid change in these relative proportions.

Estimates of unemployment vary considerably. The government's New Employment Policy (1995) cites an overall unemployment rate of 13 per cent. Unemployment in the 15–19 age group was close to 40 per cent in urban areas (Dar, 1995: 17). The end of guaranteed employment in the state sector and the continued slow growth of the formal economy may have ushered in a period of growing unemployment among the more educated. Certainly there is plenty of anecdotal evidence to this effect, particularly among arts and social science graduates.

Implications for UDSM & the ITP

Although the democratic transition is relatively slow, Tanzania has so far managed to avoid the political crises and violence that have accompanied the dismantling of hegemonic, one-party states elsewhere. Although clear regional–ethnic inequalities are in evidence in formal education[6] and employment, the religious dimension gives rise to major concern over the future stability of the country.[7]

59

Secondly, financial and fiscal discipline has yet to translate into rapid and sustained economic growth and employment creation.[8] Though government spending on higher education has increased significantly even under a strict fiscal regime, there is no guarantee that this will be sustained. Higher education's comparatively heavy dependence on state subsidies makes the sector particularly vulnerable in this respect.[9]

Thirdly, the current and planned rapid expansion of higher education enrolments will increase pressures on official budgets, including the need to recruit more staff. The poor performance of primary and secondary education outlined above has led to fears that the overall quality of future students and new members of staff may fall to unacceptable levels (see below).

Higher education policy

Tanzania's *Development Vision 2025* proposes 'a well-educated and learning society' as one of five major attributes. The others are 'a high-quality livelihood; peace, stability and unity; good governance'; and a 'competitive economy capable of producing sustainable growth and shared benefits'. Education and knowledge will instil 'a developmental mindset and competitive spirit' (URT, Planning Commission, 1999: 3–4).

The national *Higher Education Policy* (1999) lists the major problems facing higher education in Tanzania:

- appallingly low student enrolment;
- gross imbalance in science relative to liberal arts;
- gender imbalance;
- poor financing;
- unregulated, uncontrolled proliferation of tertiary training institutions;
- a tendency to distort the real worth of academic programmes.

A number of strategies have been proposed to address these problems. For example, higher enrolments can be achieved by expanding public facilities and encouraging private universities, cost sharing, affirmative action to expand female participation,

---

Box 7: Vision 2025

Tanzania's development vision is to graduate 'from a least developed country to a middle income country with a high level of human development, by the year 2025'. Education is seen as 'a strategic change agent for mindset transformation...' To solve the 'development challenges ahead, the education system should be restructured and transformed qualitatively with a focus on promoting creativity and problem solving'. A strong economy and good governance are the main preconditions for realizing the vision. Other highlights are the following.

Tanzania will brace itself to attain 'a high level of quality of education in order to respond to development challenges and effectively compete regionally and internationally [as] competitive leadership in the 21st century will hinge on the level and quality of education and knowledge'.

Tanzania should be a nation with '[a] high level of education ...; a nation which produces the quantity and quality of educated people sufficiently equipped with the requisite knowledge to solve the society's problems, meet the challenges of development and attain competitiveness at regional and global levels.

'Basic sciences and mathematics must be accorded signal importance in keeping with the demands of the modern technological age. Science and technology education and awareness of its applications for promoting and enhancing productivity should permeate the whole society through continuous learning and publicity campaigns.'

Information and communication technologies ... are a major driving force for the realization of the Vision.

Source: URT, Planning Commission (1999).

more non-residential places, efficiency gains and distance education. Although the policy favours increased official funding for higher education, the idea of an earmarked education tax, mooted elsewhere as a means of 'ring-fencing' education spending, is not mentioned.

Higher education curricula should be:

geared towards ... the changing world of science and technology and the corresponding ever-changing needs of the people, their government, industry, commerce and the surrounding environment in general. As agriculture will continue to be the backbone of the economy, agriculture-related disciplines and technologies shall be given priority (URT, MSTHE, 1999).

Training and research objectives will target the development and promotion of a strong indigenous base of science and technology to enable Tanzanians to solve their development problems.

The policy is broadly similar to that contained in *The Education and Training Policy* (URT, MOEC, 1995) summarized in Appendix 1. Many of the policy recommendations are expected to be incorporated in the draft Higher Education Act, discussed below.

Implications for the ITP
University enrolments: growth, quality & equity concerns

The policy during the 1970s favouring the growth of primary at the expense of secondary education meant that the number of high-school graduates qualifying for university places was severely constrained. UDSM enrolments tripled between 1967 and 1976, from 711 to 2,145 students (Sanyal and Kinunda, 1977). Thereafter expansion virtually ceased: between 1984 and 1993, UDSM enrolments rose only from 2,913 to 2,968,

Table 6: University undergraduate enrolment in Tanzania, 1985–2000 [a]

	1985/6	1995/6	1996/7	1997/8	1998/9	1999/2000
UDSM	2,987	3,544	3,770	4,131	4,172	4,816
MUCHS	–	357	379	443	548	626
UCLAS	–	–	91	463	501	728
SUA	480	1,100	1,040	1,253	1,300	1,425
Others	–	–	–	–	–	1,459
Total	3,467	5,001	5,280	6,290	6,521	9,054

Note: a) OUT, which is not included in this table, has about 6,700 registered students. Estimate by Prof. G. Mmari (pers. comm.) updating Ishumi et al., 2000: 2.
Source: URT, MSTHE (2000).

less than 2 per cent (USDM, 1995b: 12). By 1990, Tanzania had only 3,146 students attending its two universities, less than one-tenth of the number in Kenya (Cooksey and Riedmiller, 1997). Enrolments in the Sokoine University of Agriculture (SUA) actually fell, from 465 in 1986 to 383 in 1990 (URT, MOEC, 1991: 27). The slow growth in enrolments in Tanzanian higher education contrasts with the trends in sub-Saharan Africa overall, where enrolments grew by over 60 per cent during the 1980s (Saint, 1992: xii).

More recently, total enrolments rose sharply. New universities opened, and existing ones increased their student intake. Table 6 shows the overall trend.

New private universities are in the process of registration with the newly established Higher Education Accreditation Council. The Catholic Church operates Augustine University (Mwanza), and the Lutheran Church owns Tumaini University, with campuses in Arusha, Iringa and Moshi. There are two private medical universities, both in Dar es Salaam,

63

Table 7: UDSM undergraduate enrolments 1999–2000, by degree & gender

Course	Male	Female	Total	Male %	Female %
B.A. General	740	350	1,090	68	32
B.A. Education	365	202	567	64	36
B.Ed. (PESC)	69	30	99	70	30
B.Ed.	102	77	179	57	43
B.Commerce	476	112	588	81	19
LLB	348	193	541	64	36
B.Sc. Engineering	853	49	902	95	5
B.Sc. General	122	62	184	66	34
B.Sc. Comp. with/IN	122	10	132	92	8
B.Sc. Electrical	49	3	52	94	6
B.Sc. Geology	75	5	80	94	6
B.Sc. Education	279	122	401	70	30
Total main campus	3,600	1,215	4,815	75	25
M.D.	333	102	435	76	24
D.D.S.	57	20	77	74	26
B.Pharmacy	67	38	105	64	36
B.Sc. Nursing	16	18	34	47	53
Total MUCHS	473	178	651	73	27
B.Architecture	117	10	127	92	8
B.Sc.Be.	156	19	175	89	11
B.Sc.URP	73	18	91	80	20
B.Sc.LS	89	9	98	91	9
B.Sc.LMV	97	18	115	84	16
B.Sc.EE	104	17	121	86	14
Total UCLAS	636	91	727	87	13
Grand total	4,709	1,484	6,193	76	24

Source: UDSM, *Facts and Figures 1999/2000.*

Table 8: UDSM actual & projected undergraduate enrolment, 1997–2003

Faculty	1997–8	2002–03	% increase
Arts and social sciences	1,538	2,040	33
Commerce and management	509	1,170	130
Education	100	875	775
Engineering	805	2,367	194
Law	345	815	136
Science	793	1,558	96
Total main campus	4,090	8,825	116
MUCHS	446	970	117
UCLAS	463	880	90
Total	4,999	10,675	117

Source: Adapted from UDSM, *Facts and Figures 1999/2000*: 56–8.

and one public and two private universities planned for Zanzibar. Bukoba University is described as semi-private. Other universities are planned by upgrading various existing post-secondary training institutes. Yet other planned colleges have religious or private sponsors.

Forty per cent of students attending Tumaini University are female, a very creditable performance, given that men almost exclusively take the major courses in theology and divinity. A quarter of Zanzibar University (business administration and law) students are female, which is about the same percentage as that at UDSM. Figures on gender balance are not available for other colleges.

As well as degree courses, the new universities also offer diplomas in nursing, accountancy and journalism, among other subjects (URT, Higher Education Accreditation Council, 2000).

65

Recently, undergraduate numbers have grown rapidly at UDSM. Between 1992 and 1999, first-year admissions rose from 883 to 2,055, an increase of 133 per cent. The number of graduates also started to rise. The main campus and MUCHS produced 777 graduates in 1992, rising to 1,167 in 1998, an increase of 50 per cent. During the same period, the number of postgraduate degrees awarded increased from 110 to 126 (UDSM, *Facts and Figures 1999/2000*: 51, 54–5). A more detailed breakdown of recent UDSM enrolments by course is given in Table 7.

Table 8 shows actual enrolments for 1997–8 and projections for undergraduate enrolments by the academic year 2002–03.

With the exception of FASS, all faculties expect to expand rapidly during the next few years.

Does expansion help the poor & disadvantaged?

There are no data on trends in the recruitment of disadvantaged students at UDSM, but a few general points are in order. The relevant dimensions of inequality are gender, religion, ethnicity, culture and class. These are interrelated in multiple ways.

More students with 'A' level certificates means a growing pool of potential university students. University expansion will absorb a growing number of school leavers with the minimum entry qualifications. However, it is not self-evident that expanding undergraduate enrolments at UDSM and other Tanzanian universities will significantly improve the educational opportunities for the children of the poor, girls and non-Christian students.

As noted earlier, the FCM tracer study found that over two-fifths of former students sampled were from two regions only, Kilimanjaro (26 per cent) and Kagera (15 per cent). Two-thirds came from only six of Tanzania's 22 regions. The sample consisted of 85 per cent Christians and 14 per cent Muslims; 22 per cent were women (Kaijage, 2000: 20, 22–3).

Gender dimension

Less than a quarter of UDSM undergraduates are female. Science and engineering subjects enrol many fewer female students than arts and social sciences. Female students comprised 17 per cent of first-year admissions on the main campus in 1992–3, rising to 26 per cent during the 2000–01. For MUCHS, the comparable figures were 28.3 and 27.0 per cent. Female students accounted for 15.4 per cent of UCLAS's first intake in 1996, falling to 11.7 per cent in 2000. Women accounted for 20 per cent of OUT's new students in 1999 (Open University of Tanzania, 1999: 1). Thus, trends in gender-based selection during the recent period of expansion show some gains and some setbacks for female students.

Of the 804 Tanzanian students obtaining postgraduate degrees between 1992 and 1998, only 20 per cent were female, with large variations between arts and science (UDSM, 1999a: 55). Although exact figures are not available, the majority of female students were Christian, with a disproportionate number coming from Kilimanjaro Region.

The university has already taken some practical measures to promote an increased number of female students:

- lowering the entry cut-off point by 1.5 points for women;
- conducting a pre-entry programme for women wanting to join science-based programmes;
- giving a tuition waiver of 20 per cent to female students who join the university under the Human Resources Development Trust Fund scheme operating in the Faculty of Engineering;
- giving women priority in campus accommodation.[10]

Diluting student quality?

Whether this expansion implies a dilution in the qualifications of first-year students depends on trends in secondary-school outputs in the appropriate disciplines (number and standard of

67

'A' level passes) and the discriminatory powers of the selection process (are 'A' levels and UDSM selection procedures working efficiently?). Another factor might be the number of fee-paying students, who for the moment are still very few.

Following claims of examination irregularities and the forging of examination certificates, 1999–2000 first-year students on the main campus were given a number of tests, in English, maths, general knowledge and their 'A' level subjects of specialization. Although the results have not yet been made public, it seems that performance was generally quite reasonable. In future, the matriculation examination will be used to select first-year entrants after an initial screening of students' 'A' level results.

Detailed analysis of these factors is beyond the scope of the present review, but a few empirical observations are in order.

The number of 'A' level candidates was 5,032 in 1991, rising to 6,867 in 1995 and 9,593 in 1998. In the latter year, just over 6,000 students obtained divisions I–III in their Advanced Certificates and 2,310 obtained divisions I and II. In 1999, UDSM's three campuses combined enrolled just over 2,000 new students,[11] and SUA, a further 608 (URP, MOEC, 1996: 21; 1997: 31; 1999: 48; UDSM, 2000a; SUA, 1997).

The older generation of UDSM staff and administrators shares the belief that the academic standards of school leavers and university students have fallen steadily over the years, reflecting the overall declining quality of the national education system. Students, they feel, are particularly lacking in command of written and spoken English.

The academic audit observed that students exhibited problems of speaking, writing and self-expression in English. Moreover, the audit said that 'English will be equally problematic among teachers as the university will be compelled to recruit young staff in the face of a massive exit (retiring) of the current older teaching cadre in the next four or five years' (UDSM, 1999a: 8).

Many older faculty members are of the opinion that the new generation of university teachers is broadly lacking in the basic skills required for intellectual leadership. Since such perceptions are typical between the generations, they have to be assessed with care, but there is clearly real cause for concern.

The HIV/AIDS situation at UDSM

Global HIV/AIDS statistics as well as statistics from the Tanzanian Ministry of Health indicate that about half of the newly-infected are in the 15–34 age range, which is quite similar to the UDSM student age group. The HIV/AIDS situation in Tanzania is worse than that of North and West Africa and better than that of Southern Africa. As is well known, two-thirds of the world's HIV/AIDS cases are in sub-Saharan Africa.

At UDSM, between 1986 and 1999 there were 40 reported AIDS cases among students and 106 among staff. The cumulative deaths from HIV/AIDS-related causes among students at the main campus and staff members were 16 and 49 respectively. While these are only the reported cases, they have had a severe impact on the university, although the impact has not been quantified. The situation requires prudent control measures. The negative effects of HIV/AIDS include:

- loss of investments in human capital;
- loss of the only available professionals in certain disciplines;
- increased workloads for faculty due to an increased student–staff ratio;
- loss of work hours through death or illness;
- social stigma resulting in dropouts or even suicide;
- increased social welfare and medical costs.

The university has established preventive and intervention programmes in response to the alarming situation, namely:

69

- preventive and curative services at the University Health Centre;
- the University Health Education Programme;
- the university-based Youth Reproductive Health Programme.

Although these efforts have helped to enhance awareness about HIV/AIDS, they are far from sufficient. Much more needs to be done, given the magnitude of the problem. Among the obstacles faced in these efforts, even at university level, are the cultural taboos forbidding open discussion of sexual behaviour.

Changes in the legal framework
Proposed legislation

The University of Dar es Salaam Act No. 12 of 1970, dating from its establishment, is regarded as a major constraint in bringing about desired institutional changes. The Act was designed on the premise of state control, single-party politics and a monolithic party ideology. Section 4(a) of the Act still states that 'The objects and functions of the University shall be to preserve, transmit and enhance knowledge for the benefit of the people of Tanzania in accordance with the principles of socialism accepted by the people of Tanzania.'

Realizing that the Act is outdated, the university has been working on various fronts to amend it radically or to replace it with another act designed to meet the challenges of the present and future. The fast-changing socio-economic environment and the revised mission, objectives, functions, strategies and long-term plan of the UDSM require an appropriate legal framework in order to acquire validity and legitimacy. To this effect, the Ministry of Science, Technology and Higher Education and the university have jointly proposed a draft bill, frequently referred to as the 'university umbrella act'.

The proposed bill, on its way to parliament, includes:

- a broadening, revising and expansion of the objectives and functions of the university to reflect its new vision, policies and strategies;
- provision for a flexible university act that accords the university increased external and internal autonomy in such strategic aspects as appointments, governance, financial management, enrolment growth rates, structural reforms and policy issues;
- recognition of the public nature of the institution without hindering it from developing strategic alliances with various stakeholders in areas crucial to its development and self-sustenance, such as delivery of its programmes as well as the funding and marketing of its products;
- creation of relevant institutional mechanisms to enable the UDSM to respond in timely fashion to rapid socio-economic changes.

Resource mobilization

The proposed umbrella act provides for the establishment of a grants committee, one of whose functions would be to increase access to higher-education institutions through the development of new sources of funding for such institutions, especially for women, the disabled and other disadvantaged groups (URT, 1998: 20).

Membership of the Council

According to the proposed bill, membership of the University Council shall not be less than ten and not more than 15. Eight of them are mentioned explicitly in the proposed act, namely:

- the chairman, to be appointed by the President;
- the Vice-Chancellor, as an *ex-officio* member;
- two members of the National Assembly;

71

- one member appointed by the MSTHE;
- one member appointed by the minister in charge of education;
- one member appointed by the minister in charge of finance;
- one member appointed by the Government of Zanzibar.

The rest of the members are to be appointed in accordance with relevant regulations.

Commission of Higher Education

The proposed act provides for the establishment of a Commission of Higher Education whose functions would include:

- promoting the objectives of higher education;
- auditing on a regular basis to ensure the quality of higher education;
- promoting cooperation among higher-education institutions in Tanzania.

The proposed act also provides for the establishment of a Committee of Vice-Chancellors, Principals and Directors that would have a vital role to play in the affairs of the Higher Education Commission.

Selection of the Vice-Chancellor & other officials

The 1970 Act provides for the appointment of most key administrative officers (Vice-Chancellor, CACO and CADO, deans and directors) by the President in his role as Chancellor. The 1990 amendment to the Act separated the function of president from that of chancellor. Consequently, all but the three top officials became appointees of the Chancellor. The top three are still presidential appointees, with appointments for an indefinite period. In the proposed new act, all key administrative officers are appointed by the Council for a definite period of tenure (Nyirwa, 2000). The new act specifies their identification by a research committee or from public advertisement. Under the proposed act, the President appoints only the Chancellor and the Chairman, for a definite period of tenure.

It should be noted that the proposed act makes no mention of gender.

Notes

1   Appendix 4 provides some key socio-economic indicators.
2   Peter sees some improvements in the lobbying capacity of civil-society groups in the intervening years (pers. comm., 2000).
3   The government's target is to eliminate absolute poverty by the year 2025 and to reduce it to half its current level by 2010 (URT, Vice President's Office, 1998).
4   See Appendix 1 for excerpts from the 1995 *Education and Training Policy*.
5   These figures ignore the undeclared (often substantial) income of some, particularly senior, government and parastatal employees.
6   See above and Appendix 5 for primary and secondary levels and the following discussion for UDSM.
7   The closure of UDSM for an entire academic year (1991) was in part the result of personalized attacks on President Mwinyi, a Zanzibari Muslim, by a largely Christian, mainland-origin student body.
8   Agricultural export performance has been particularly disappointing.
9   Dependence on donors for investment in infrastructure and research is, presumably, unsustainable in the longer term. Past failures to match recurrent expenditure to capital investment have led to poor plant maintenance; current major donor-funded investments run the same risk.
10 Female students now occupy several accommodation blocks previously occupied by male students.
11 Further information on SUA is in Appendix 2.

5 Unfinished Business

Initially the reform process at the University of Dar es Salaam concentrated on reforming the financial and administrative structures as well as the legal framework supporting those structures. Since 1998, reform efforts have extended to include the academic plant itself. The first step in this direction was the undertaking of the academic audit exercise in 1998–9. Currently the university is striving to implement recommendations emanating from the academic audit.

Although reform of the financial, administrative and legal structures and procedures will continue to be important features of the programme, there is no doubt that the future reforms will focus mainly on the academic structures and processes which constitute the core business of a university. The unfinished business of the reform process will therefore concentrate on such issues as what is being taught, how it is being taught, who is teaching it, who is being taught, in what environment, with what effect and what is the overall impact on the needs and requirements of the broader society.

These critical issues of reform are addressed and highlighted in four important documents, namely, the *Report of the 1998 Academic Audit* (1999a), the *Five-Year Rolling Strategic Plans of Colleges, Faculties and Institutes* (1999), the *University-Level Five-Year Rolling Strategic Plan 2000–04* (1999) and the *Proposed Priority Future Support Areas for UDSM* (1999a). (The first three documents have already been discussed.)

These documents and others, as well as interviews with directly concerned individuals and a meeting of the ITP Steering Committee, are the sources for the discussion of unfinished business that follows. We think that directing funding to activities falling within the following areas will greatly help in enhancing the reform process and propelling it forward.

Improving the teaching-learning process

There is wide consensus on the need to step up efforts to improve the effectiveness of teaching and learning. A number of important and pertinent measures have been suggested, such as enhancement of computer literacy among staff and students, increasing accessibility to computer use and the internet, production of relevant and up-to-date textbook materials, enhancement of library facilities and networking. However, the most fundamental measure that would give a base to all the other measures would seem to be the carrying out of systematic tracer studies to determine the adequacy and relevance of curricula and programmes (see Research priorities section below).

Our position is based on two factors. First, the rapid political, economic and social changes that began in the early 1990s have changed the identity of Tanzania so radically that many of the assumptions that inspired and informed the present curricula and programmes are no longer valid. Secondly, Tanzania has in the meantime developed a long-term national vision, *Vision 2025*, (discussed above) in which a number of important issues and principles are articulated and highlighted as guiding pillars for future development effort. Well-conducted tracer studies should be able to uncover systematic gaps and anomalies in human resources development that the university can address by revisiting its curricula and programmes.

Along with the tracer studies, special attention should also be paid to the ability of students to learn. Even if the curricula and programmes are adequate and relevant and the delivery perfect, the ability of the learner to benefit maximally from such programmes is crucial. Evidence gathered suggests that the students' ability to learn effectively is poor, partly because of English language difficulties. Resources should be spent on discovering the source and nature of the students' weak capacity to learn and on taking appropriate steps to remedy the situation. Blaming the earlier years of schooling is not helpful. Ways should be found to help those who are at the university today so that they can benefit maximally from what is being offered to them.

Staff development

A university is as good as the quality of its staff. Although the University of Dar es Salaam can boast of a good number of doctorate holders, they are concentrated in certain academic areas, and many of them will soon reach retirement age. A recruitment freeze in the 1990s has left the university vulnerable with respect to succession and continuity in teaching and research. If the ITP is not to falter, it is important for the university to embark on a massive recruitment and training drive. Special attention should be paid to new fields of enquiry that are relevant to the country's new vision and to important traditional fields that failed to attract adequate staff in the past. The university and the government should also consider putting in place incentives that will motivate good staff to remain with the university.

The staff development effort should address the following categories of training:

- doctorate training for academic staff;
- master's degrees for both academic and technical staff;
- short-term training and exchange programmes for academic, technical and administrative staff;
- continuing professional education programmes for all staff, plus sabbaticals to enable academic staff to keep abreast of the rapid changes in knowledge content, structure and delivery systems.

Developing more efficient management tools

One of the recommendations of the academic audit report was the decentralization and rationalization of academic units at

different levels. The efficient management of relatively autonomous units calls for better tools of coordination and discrete
control. A Management Information System needs to be set up
in order to equip management with reliable information for
decision-making on all aspects of the institution. Along with
this, it will also be useful to develop a multi-purpose smart-
card system to facilitate the processing of a number of activities
such as registration, examinations and library access. Further-
more, the library needs to be upgraded and better equipped in
order to meet the ever-growing needs of the academic
community.

Organizational structure

Reform of the university's organizational structure remains on
the agenda. A recent report on the organizational structure of
UDSM identifies several problems inherent in the present
structure (UDSM, 1999b).

- it is excessively centralized;
- it divides the workforce into two potentially competing
  camps, one under the CACO and the other under the
  CADO;
- it relies heavily on committees for decision-making which
  has a bad impact on efficient and effective management;
- the span of control for the offices of CACO and CADO is too
  wide by international standards, thereby undermining their
  efficiency and effectiveness.

The report proposes a new organizational structure designed
to eliminate these weaknesses, with three deputy Vice-
Chancellors, responsible for (a) teaching, research and consultancy; (b) planning, finance and development; and (c) human
resources management and general administration. The new
organizational structure is influenced and guided by four

important documents, namely the MSTHE's *Higher Education Policy*, the Higher Education Accreditation Council's *Applications to Establish Higher Education Institutions in Tanzania*, the proposed University of Dar es Salaam Act and the UDSM *Corporate Strategic Plan*. The MSTHE policy document sets the general guidelines for the standards to be met before an institution is accorded the status of a university. The Higher Education Accreditation Council document spells out the role of the Council as a watchdog of the government in matters relating to quality and accreditation. The proposed UDSM Act defines the legitimate positions of the university's managers, confers the desired authority on these positions, delineates the type of staff that can be engaged and empowers certain organs to make binding decisions that can affect the management of the university. The *Corporate Strategic Plan* defines one of the objectives of the ITP as having an institution that is free from excessive external control.

Some of the features of the proposed structure, which are very much in line with the proposed umbrella university act, are as follows:

- a high degree of decentralization of duties and decision-making to colleges and faculties;
- further strengthening of financial and administrative functions at faculty levels;
- recomposition of Council, Senate and college management boards and a more comprehensive articulation of their powers;
- introduction of a departmental board;
- clearer articulation of lines of accountability and responsibility; and
- an enhanced and integrated approach to institutional planning, finance, development and management.

Infrastructure development

Although not many donors are interested in funding physical structures, physical infrastructure is necessary for carrying out academic functions. The expansion of academic programmes and the growth of student enrolment both require the provision of additional space. Space utilization is currently at 80 per cent. New structures that are badly needed include laboratories, workshops and lecture theatres, the sanitation infrastructure, sports facilities and student centres for both the main campus and the constituent colleges.

The location of the UDSM main campus and UCLAS – 16 kilometres from the town centre – is a disadvantage in that the university cannot attract people for parallel degree programmes, which have proved to be popular and revenue-generating at Makerere and Nairobi universities. For the university to run successful parallel undergraduate pro-grammes, it must procure premises close to the centre of town. This will provide a reliable source of additional income for the university, while at the same time providing access to higher education for a larger segment of the population.

Research priorities

Undertaking the following studies is essential to the success of institutional reform and transformation at UDSM.

Full-scale, university-wide tracer study

Such a study was proposed earlier in the context of essential measures to improve the effectiveness of teaching and learning. We return to it in the context of research studies. From this perspective a university-wide tracer study would:

- document trends in the employment status of and oppor-tunities for graduates;

79

- report employers' views on graduates' skills, learning potential and attitudes to work; and
- look at graduates' perceptions of their own strengths and weaknesses as employees and attitudes to self-employment.

The results would also provide UDSM with vital information on the quality of undergraduate training programmes and attempts to improve the quality and relevance of teaching and learning. This study should be managed independently of the individual colleges, faculties and departments, to assure the objectivity of the results. This should not preclude active cooperation with individual departments and staff. Since there has been no attempt to date to undertake a university-wide tracer study, the results could provide an important baseline for follow-up studies to chart trends in graduate employment, self-employment and employability. Resources permitting, such a tracer study could also include SUA and OUT.

Study of the financial sustainability of the ITP
After years of stagnation, UDSM enrolments are again expanding rapidly. Current large donor-funded investments in teaching facilities and ICT have significant implications for future recurrent budgets. The cost of research is funded largely from external sources. The physical plant, including staff accommodation, is inadequately maintained. Consultancies largely benefit individuals, not the university. Numerous opportunities for privatizing non-core functions still exist. Many income-generating opportunities have not yet been fully exploited. More has been done to date in Tanzania in this area at primary and secondary levels. By international standards, UDSM is still highly dependent on government subventions that carry no long-term guarantees. The proposed study would model various financial scenarios based on projections of student enrolments, income from all sources (the state, donors,

students and the private sector) and the cost of running the university on a sustainable basis.

Evaluation of the relevance & impact of research undertaken at UDSM

The importance of deepening synergies between university research and national development, including poverty reduction, is widely recognized. Yet there is little evidence to suggest that these linkages are becoming more effective in influencing government or donor agency policies, strategies, programmes or projects, or in informing the public on major development issues. Although the development relevance and impact of much basic research cannot be easily demonstrated in the short term, much applied research can and should be judged from these perspectives. UDSM's dependence on foreign research funding makes it vulnerable to cuts in aid budgets, and the university would benefit from demonstrating concern with enhancing relevance and impact. If the effect of research were assessed, it would facilitate the prioritizing of research for funding based on previous performance.

Study on equity and the ITP

A more market-driven approach to higher education may have negative consequences on equity. Little is known about past and present trends in undergraduate recruitment in terms of gender, class, regional origin, ethnicity, religion or disability. A university-wide study would help document the success of the current gender initiatives and inform future 'positive discrimination' policies promoting increased access for disadvantaged groups.

Determination of how to generate and sustain support for the ITP

The university has invested much time and effort in 'selling' the ITP to academic staff and students. Yet, as recent events in the FOE demonstrate, the question remains of whether

81

administrative and academic staff and students have assimilated the implications of the trend away from state-controlled and -funded higher education towards a more market-oriented model. Are they prepared to take up the challenges posed by new information technologies? An investigation of public perceptions of the role of the university in the twenty-first century would be an important addition to this research. The views of politicians and policy-makers are also highly relevant to generating support for an institutionalized ITP.

Improving the annual Facts and Figures *publication*
Facts and Figures needs to be more user-friendly. A small panel study of end-users of the present *Facts and Figures* would establish areas for improvement in terms of:

- areas covered;
- regularity of coverage;
- the utility of the information provided, particularly the kinds of data disaggregations presented;
- the reliability and validity of the data.

ICT

Among the steps that could be taken to promote effective use of ICT at the university are:

- computers need to be widely available for students, faculty and staff;
- lecturers should require their students to carry out CD-ROM and internet literature searches in preparation for research projects;
- users need better CD-ROM and internet training – not just on using the technologies but also in information retrieval skills. Researchers need to know how to phrase search

queries and how to evaluate search results;
*   an information retrieval skills cluster should be added to research methodology courses, to be team-taught by a librarian and a lecturer;
*   students need to learn how to type properly if they are to become active users of computers and ICT. A typing-tutor programme should be installed on the campus network.

Conclusion

The University of Dar es Salaam has managed to take bold decisions and put in place firm measures that have enabled it not only to stop the process of decay that had afflicted the institution before the reform process began, but also to gear up to fulfil its core functions better. Unity and commitment within the university leadership and support from government and the donor community have contributed to the achievements attained so far. If this partnership can be maintained and strengthened in order to tackle the unfinished business pointed out above, then there is every hope that the university will succeed in its bid to regain its former glory as a centre of academic excellence.

At the same time, there is no room for complacency. The fruits of the reforms initiated with the ITP have yet to be fully harvested. The rapid expansion of enrolment that is under way will inevitably stretch the human and physical resources of the university and threaten to undermine the quality improvements that are being planned. It is encouraging to see that the university administration is already looking seriously at the employability of graduates, with a major tracer study under way, as recommended in this report. The UDSM's ability to produce employable graduates is the ultimate test of the ITP.

The long-term maintenance of any good-quality institution depends on funding and how it is used. Continued heavy dependence on capital investments from donors will exacerbate the sustainability issue unless organizational and curriculum innovations result in increased operating funds and gains in efficiency. By international standards, the level of private financing of Tanzanian higher education, including the UDSM, is rather low. The involvement of donors in recurrent cost activities, including research, puts added stress on limited resources and absorptive capacity. Senior academics are lured into the world of NGOs, consultancy and working for government and donors, leaving a major gap in the professorial ranks that cannot be filled in the short term without recruiting expatriate teachers or consultants.

Confronting these issues will require clear thinking and continued innovation on the part of the university leadership, a working relationship with government and well-targeted donor support. Balancing continued growth in student enrolment with improvements in quality constitutes the major challenge for the UDSM in the twenty-first century.

Appendix 1

Excerpts from the Education & Training Policy

The 1995 Education and Training Policy stresses the liberalization and expansion of higher education, as well as cost sharing and continued international cooperation. 'In the wake of liberalization, increased demand for middle- and high-level manpower and the social demand for higher education, ... the establishment and ownership of tertiary and higher education and training institutions shall be liberalized'.

Noting the comparatively low level of Tanzanian university and other post-secondary enrolments, the policy states that 'Enrolment at universities and other institutions of higher education and training shall be increased'.

The policy also proposes greater financial contributions from parents (cost sharing), students (loans) and institutions (sale of services). The rationale for this is that overreliance on state funding has resulted in 'inadequate resources, low enrolments, high unit costs, institutional inefficiency, student unrest, non-accountability and laxity'.

Finally, in order to bridge the 'knowledge gap between ... countries of the North and those of the South ... Tanzania is committed to ... international cooperation by information sharing, exchange of professionals, students and publications. International cooperation in matters of education and training shall be encouraged and promoted.'

Source: URT, MOEC, *The Education and Training Policy*, 1995: 76–80.

Appendix 2

Sokoine University of Agriculture (SUA)

Sokoine University of Agriculture (SUA) has been an independent university since 1984. Located in Morogoro, four hours by road from Dar es Salaam, SUA has 228 academic staff providing undergraduate and postgraduate training. SUA consists of Faculties of Agriculture, Veterinary Medicine, Forestry and Nature Conservation, a recently upgraded Faculty of Science, the Institute of Continuing Education (ICE), the Centre for Sustainable Rural Development (CSRD) and the Development Studies Institute (DSI). SUA also has its own 2,000-ha farm. Over the years, donor support and institutional links have been substantial, with NORAD currently the largest donor.

A large multi-disciplinary research programme (US$6.25 million) entitled 'Food Security and Household Income for Smallholders in Tanzania' is about to take off, with funding from NORAD.

Like UDSM, SUA has embarked upon a long-term transformation process, enshrined in a *Corporate Strategic Plan* (CSP) that includes expanding student intake, improving quality and relevance in teaching and research and achieving financial sustainability. Between 1997 and 1999, first-year enrolments increased by 50 per cent, a remarkable change after years of relative stagnation in student numbers and declining government subventions. Total enrolments were 1,425 in 1999, and the Strategic Plan foresaw an expansion to 2,280 by 2000 and 4,000 by 2005, which seems excessively ambitious.

The introduction of three new undergraduate programmes accounts for all the expansion in 1998. Total enrolments in existing courses actually fell. Many students who would have enrolled in the B. Sc. agriculture course chose agricultural economics and agribusiness instead. The popularity of this and the new wildlife course reflects a growing sensitivity to emerging private-sector employment opportunities (tourism/ conservation and large-scale agriculture). Four new 'demand-driven' postgraduate programmes have also been introduced.

The expansion led to a slight decline in female participation, from 22.3 per cent in 1997 to 19.6 per cent in 1999. This parallels the experience at the UDSM. Over a third of first-year female students (36 per cent) are studying home economics and nutrition, and very few are enrolled in the three new courses.

Vision

The vision of the university for the 21st century is to be a centre of academic excellence in agricultural-related fields with emphasis on imparting skills, entrepreneurship, research and integration of basic and applied knowledge in an environmentally friendly manner for the benefit of all people.

Source: SUA, 1997.

As well as teaching and research, SUA is involved in commercial and consulting activities. Since 1992, the Institute of Continuing Education has been running short courses for professionals on natural resource management and sustainable agriculture.

Growing government and donor concerns with agriculture as a vehicle for poverty alleviation and economic growth provide SUA with strong incentives to reform its teaching, research and service functions with a view to enhancing their relevance. The introduction of demand-driven courses reflects this concern with relevance, but the need to address growth and poverty issues in smallholder agriculture through research and outreach, for which the demand will only be indirect, is equally vital. The research priority areas that are listed are too numerous to constitute real priorities.

Information on research and extension outputs is not available to assess whether SUA is successfully addressing its strategic concerns in these areas. It would be useful to trace graduates in agricultural extension to see where they are employed and how they are affected by the current trends towards privatization of agricultural research, extension, credit supply and crop marketing resulting from the growing presence of agribusiness in export crops, particularly cotton, coffee and tobacco.

Appendix 3

SIDA/SAREC Research Support
to UDSM & MUCHS

Background

SIDA is the oldest and, in terms of total funding, most significant donor to the UDSM. SAREC is the SIDA department responsible for research cooperation. SAREC finances activities in a number of research universities in the South as well as thematic programmes through regional institutions. Long-term cooperation between UDSM (including UCLAS), MUCHS and a number of Swedish research institutions is the basis of SAREC support. SAREC assists research with individual and institutional grants. In addition, it supports research equipment and libraries. With support from SAREC, 43 PhD students were in training in 1998. Research on HIV/AIDS (at MUCHS) and marine resources (at the Institute of Marine Sciences) is the largest component of SAREC support. Thematic PhD training programmes target the Faculty of Commerce and Management and UCLAS. Swedish support is worth SEK80.5 million (US$9 million) to UDSM/UCLAS and SEK31 million (US$3.5 million) to MUCHS for the 1998–2000 period, making SIDA/SAREC the largest single donor to both institutions.

SAREC research support dates back to 1976. Support for the national research council (UTAFITI) ended after a 1985 evaluation cited lack of experienced researchers in UTAFITI and a tendency for the council to act 'as a political and bureaucratic filter'. A second phase of support to individual researchers or research groups 'led to a fragmented situation' (SIDA, 1999: 2). The current phase of support to UDSM and MUCHS took off in the early 1990s and coincided with the launch of the ITP, which SIDA/SAREC has actively supported. A 1998 agreement emphasizes the role of UDSM's 'management structures in making strategies and priorities for the research cooperation' (SIDA, 1999: 2).

Relevance

SAREC's self-assessment states that it has contributed 'to produce research results of relevance to development in

89

Tanzania', citing the following examples: electric power distribution; the environmental consequences of gold mining and farming; coastal management; entrepreneurship; HIV/AIDS; and reproductive health (SIDA, 1999: 2). Other contributions include research capacity-building at UDSM and MUCHS, helping to set up structures for research management (academic and financial) and building laboratories, including the installation of scientific equipment.

Is SAREC-funded research sensitive to poverty issues? Overall, poverty alleviation is not an overarching concern for SAREC. Swedish researchers preparing proposals are advised to address priority objectives including poverty, as expounded in various policy documents. It is not clear if the Tanzanian side is exposed to this procedure to the same extent.

Apart from the poverty focus, a number of Swedish development assistance objectives are reflected in the range of research activities that are currently financed: gender, economic growth/improved livelihoods, human resource development through basic services, HIV/AIDS, environmental sustainability and (more recently) urbanization.

AIDS research, which is SAREC's largest bilateral programme, started in 1986. According to SAREC:

The scientific information resulting from the programme has been a major source of information for Tanzanian authorities setting the priorities for the National Aids Control Programme as well as for WHO's international surveillance of the AIDS pandemic and has also served to increase possibilities in and improve quality in laboratory diagnosis of HIV infection ... The external evaluation performed during early 1996 was extremely favourable (SIDA, n.d.: 4).

Support to the Faculty of Education for the Basic Education Renewal Research Initiative for Poverty Alleviation (BERRIPA) should be linked to ongoing policy-making and programming in the MOEC. Yet no senior MOEC official attended the

BERRIPA conference, organized jointly by the FOE and the Department of Human Geography, University of Goteborg (held in Arusha, November 1999). The comparative advantage of the Swedish partners in education research is not self-evident. Partnership issues discussed related to links between local and foreign researchers via the Elimu Leadership Institute, which is based on national chapters, and not to research on Tanzanian education. This appears to be an example of externally-driven research with little or no local ownership. To be fair, the focus of the faculty is on staff development, not research *per se*.

Is SAREC-funded research contributing to national development, policy debate and advocacy? Both SAREC and Tanzanian researchers consider academic and intellectual freedom important principles in determining what kind of research is undertaken. One interpretation of academic freedom would find it illegitimate to require research to have explicit practical objectives such as poverty alleviation. Basic research may or may not turn out to have long-term developmental relevance, so the argument goes. SAREC might argue that the extent to which research helps inform development policy and debate is partly a function of the disposition and motives of Tanzanian academics, over which SAREC has no control.

However, applied research should have practical spin-offs, for example in environmental engineering and technological fields. SAREC supports the Faculty of Engineering in research on electrical engineering designed to help TANESCO improve power distribution and utilization. One component of this research is studying the materials used for transmission that have been developed for use in cold climates, not the tropics. Other SAREC support with practical implications includes research on mercury contamination associated with small-scale mining and support for testing for poisons in fish caught in Lake Victoria.

91

Coherence

More direct linkages might be expected between research and Tanzania's current development strategy, policies and programmes. At the university level, one might want to know whether research sponsorship is sensitive to non-research components of the transformation programme and whether donor activities are adequately coordinated.

National policy linkages

SAREC is concerned with funding research that reflects national priorities. In MUCHS, for example, 'The research policy [of the college] will ensure that research priorities are within national priorities, deals [sic] with local problems, can be used to solve local problems and provide solutions to scientific questions ... Studies related to reproductive health have been 'health-service oriented, addressing questions that can be immediately useful to efficiently target scarce resources in the health care system' (SIDA, n.d.: 4, 11). This is arguably too narrow a focus, concentrating on official (government) as opposed to 'national' priorities, more broadly defined.

At a different level, one could ask whether SIDA has taken steps to channel research funds via the Treasury rather than directly to the UDSM. For SIDA/SAREC the practical issue is funding UDSM and MUCHS research through a more centralized system rather than through individual accounts for the various faculties and research institutes. Swedish and other external research collaborators are funded directly, not via the UDSM. Given UDSM's strategy of asserting its relative autonomy from the government, it is unlikely that the administration would agree to give up its partial control of external research funds. In this respect, the enclave nature of research sponsorship is likely to continue.

UDSM transformation programme linkages

Are SIDA/SAREC-supported researchers using their research

findings to improve their teaching? This is a concern for the transformation programme, but no work has been done on it.

One might also ask, for example, whether the stress on democratization in the country's programme has influenced the choice of social research methodologies favouring participatory techniques. Does SIDA's outreach to civil society include the possibility of research collaboration with non-governmental research groups?

Linkages with other donors

Are donors coordinating their efforts to avoid duplication in the financing of activities and to avoid putting too much pressure on the available administrative and research capacity? Are rates of payment for researchers harmonized? Does the tendency for donors to hire university staff to run projects and to undertake relatively well-paid consultancy work clash with the objective of SIDA/SAREC's and other donors' objective of promoting academic research? Do donors, including SIDA, attempt to hire consultants through university consultancy bureaux rather than directly?

Partnership

Partnership in the sense of collaborative research between Swedish and Tanzanian institutions and researchers has been the basis of SAREC's activities in Tanzania for the last 26 years. However, partnership has taken on an institutional development dimension only recently. The twin forces of UDSM's ITP from the early 1990s and the elaboration more recently of a broad Nordic donor–Tanzanian partnership have combined to helped further the concept of partnership as implementing a jointly negotiated set of policies and programmes.

The major role that donors have played in capital investment and support for training, teaching and research has

93

meant that the aid agencies have been closely involved in the transformation process since its inception in the early 1990s. As regards research, this has meant a move away from support to individual departments organized on a project-by-project basis to support at a more faculty and research institute level and central coordination through the Directorate of Research and Publications. Faculty funds were introduced in 1998. SAREC support to the transformation programme has included funding studies, publications and workshops and assisting with the establishment of a Directorate for postgraduate Studies, Research and Publications.

A midterm review (March 1999) identified inadequate reporting systems in UDSM and MUCHS and the system for disbursements from SIDA as causes of unnecessary delays (SIDA, 1999: 13). Attempts to introduce joint reporting systems, including finance and audit, are part of the ITP.

Linking arrangements include allocating a small proportion of all funding (10 per cent) to collaborative research between Swedish and Tanzanian academics.

Appendix 4

United Republic of Tanzania: Key Facts

Capital	Dodoma
Commercial capital	Dar es Salaam
Land area	945,000 km²
Population	>30 million
Economy	
Gross domestic product	$656 per capita (1994)
	$220 (1997)
Inflation	21% (1995)
	<10% (1999)
Exports	1980-89: $420 million p.a.
	1990-97: $525 million p.a.
Trade balance	–$456 million (1995)
	–$200 million (1999)
Foreign debt	$7 billion +
Social development	
Life expectancy	50 years
Population growth	2.8%
Poverty	50% on or below poverty line
Infant mortality rate	85/1,000
Calorific intake	+/– 2200 per person/day
Household income	Share of top 20%: 45%,
Distribution	Share of bottom 20%: 7%
School enrolments	Age 7–13: 57% (1995)
UNDP Human Development Index (1997)	0.463
	(rank 156/174)
Transparency International	1.9/10 (81st out of
Corruption Perception Index (1999)	85 countries polled)

Source: Adapted from International Cooperative Alliance, *Tanzania Cooperative Country Study* (Geneva, 1999).

Appendix 5

Tanzania: Economic, Political & Policy Transformations

Recent political & economic trends

The nature and magnitude of basic social, political and economic changes going on in the country condition the likelihood of a successful transformation process at UDSM. For example, trends in the selection of UDSM students based on gender, ethnicity, region, class and religion inevitably reflect such changes. Likewise, trends towards more representative government will affect the extent to which the political elite is prepared to loosen central government control of higher education finance and management. Economic growth affects the tax base of the country and the possibility of increasing official funding for higher education as well as the potential for cost-sharing measures. Finally, policy choices (and non-choices) influence the total revenues available for education overall and for higher education in particular, as well as the nature and extent of measures taken to reduce the recruitment inequalities mentioned above. The following sections describe these contextual factors in general terms as background for the discussion of trends in educational policy and practice.

A partial transition to democracy

Like the rest of sub-Saharan Africa, Tanzania is experiencing a period of rapid political and economic change. Heavily influenced by bilateral aid donors, the process of change encompasses both political pluralism and economic liberalization. Tanzania's starting point for these basic transitions was a highly centralized, single-party state, subservient civil-society institutions and an economy largely dominated by state-owned industrial, financial and marketing monopolies.

Following the publication of the Nyalali Report (URT, 1992), the country rapidly legalized competitive political activities, and multi-party elections were held in October 1995. The ruling CCM party was returned to power with a comfortable majority of seats in the National Assembly. Factionalism and personality

96

conflicts had weakened the major opposition parties, which did not mount a serious challenge to CCM in the October 2000 elections.

For many years a mouthpiece of the ruling party, the uni-cameral National Assembly has yet to emerge as an effective check on the powers of the executive. One important step in the right direction was the appointment of an opposition MP to head the Public Accounts Committee. Yet the PAC's critical comments on the Auditor General's annual report, which regularly reveals enormous misuse of public funds, has not led to major sanctions against senior public officials.

The relative peace and tranquillity of the Tanzanian polity means that the state does not frequently resort to systematic and violent repression. At the same time, according to one observer, 'the state/party ... are ... not prepared to change the status quo in favour of a larger democracy'. A less categorical assessment might consider the possible pitfalls of too rapid a transition to 'a larger democracy'. There are many examples, in Africa and elsewhere, where the transition to competitive politics has led to instability and violence rather than more representative and accountable government.

A constitutional review process is under way to determine, among other things, the future shape of the union between the mainland (the former Tanganyika) and Zanzibar. The so-called union question has been complicated by the unresolved political crisis in Zanzibar following the 1995 elections and plans (that eventually failed) to change the Zanzibari constitution to allow the present president of the Isles to run for a third term. Most aid to Zanzibar has been suspended, pending the trial or release of opposition leaders held in remand on accusations of treason.

According to one group of observers, the major obstacles to democratization include the reluctance of the old political class to loosen its grip on power; systematic political corruption; weak performance and capacities of the opposition parties; inadequate capacity and resources of civil society; lack of resources and quality staff in the independent media; poor facilities and resources in the judiciary; the general culture of accepting an authoritarian, hierarchical social structure; and lack of public information and knowledge of rights (Peter et al, 1995).

The same authors see little evidence of movement towards increased democracy during recent years, although there are signs of greater lobbying efforts by civil society groups. On the negative side, the Thirteenth Amendment to the constitution will strengthen the powers of the President, who will require only a simple majority to be elected and who will be given powers to nominate up to ten members of the National Assembly.

Corruption has been a major policy issue since 1994, when Benjamin Mkapa declared that fighting corruption would be a key concern of his presidency. The publication of the Warioba Report (URT, 1996) documenting systematic official corruption – both grand and petty – was followed by various government initiatives, including the sacking of a number of senior officials and revenue collectors, the strengthening of the Prevention of Corruption Bureau and the publication of a strategy and action plan. Nevertheless, there is a widespread popular view that the President lacks support for his anti-corruption strategy among top officials. Donor aid to anti-corruption and good governance initiatives is substantial.

A recent report by the US State Department maintains that 'Pervasive corruption constrains economic progress' (US Department of State 2000: 1). The three East African countries were said to have 'poor' human rights records.

With some notable exceptions, local NGOs have yet to play a major role in the democratization process. Many lack transparency, internal democracy and clear commitment to the causes they espouse. The ready availability of donor funds to promote NGOs is a mixed blessing. The concept of challenging the state's performance rather than simply implementing official policies is not readily embraced.

A partial transition to a market economy

The profound economic crisis of the late 1970s and early 1980s led to the reluctant adoption of a World Bank-IMF structural adjustment programme and the gradual abandonment of the command economy after 1985. Both internal and external factors were blamed for the crisis, but key factors included relative pricing policies, forced villagization, the uneconomic organization of crop marketing, large-scale investment in inefficient public corporations, the confinement of internal and external trade to government monopolies, and growing corruption. Depressed commodity prices are predicted to persist and export-led growth is likely to come from gold and other minerals and from tourism. Foreign direct investment in these sectors, particularly in gold mining, has picked up dramatically in recent years.

Table 9 summarizes some recent macroeconomic indicators.

Table 9: Trends in selected economic indicators, 1994–2000

Trend	Financial year				
	1994/5	1995/6	1997/8	1998/9	1999/00
GDP growth (%)	1.4	3.6	3.5	4.1	4.8
Inflation (%)	21.0	16.1	12.3	9.0	7.5
Tax/GDP (%)	11.3	12.1	11.5	11.5	11.9
Export/import ratio (%)	34.0	56.0	62.8	61.7	65.0
Balance of payments (US$m)	–456	–254	–362	–214	–200
External debt (US$m)	6,260	7,230	7,520	7,782	8,000

Source: URT, Planning Commission (1999), p.2.

Total exports averaged US$420 million per annum between 1980 and 1989, rising to US$525 million for 1990-97. During the same periods, imports averaged US$1.1 billion and US$1.5 billion, giving an export/import declining ratio from 46 per cent to 35 per cent respectively (World Bank, 1996; URT, 1998b).

99

After years of economic stagnation, gross national product (GNP) growth has picked up recently, although it is still well below the level required to make a significant dent in current poverty levels (see below). Agricultural export performance has varied between sectors. Tanzania's chronic balance-of-payments deficit is made up by donor assistance, resulting in an unsustainable external debt burden. The government's strict fiscal policy has virtually eliminated budget deficits and inflation has fallen from an average of over 30 per cent in the 1990s to single digits currently (URT, Bank of Tanzania, 1999).

Since its creation, the Tanzania Revenue Authority (TRA) has generally succeeded in meeting its revenue targets and has successfully introduced VAT to replace sales tax. However, tax collection remains unimpressive as a proportion of GDP (13 per cent) (URT, Ministry of Finance, 1999). The business community complains of harassment by TRA assessors, the high level of taxes, the proliferation of numerous 'nuisance' taxes and continued tax evasion by politically well-connected companies.

Tanzania's very poor ranking in Transparency International's annual *Corruption Perception Index* reflects the low level of confidence in the country's investment environment among both foreign and local entrepreneurs (Transparency International 1998, 1999).

At an average of nearly US$1 billion a year, aid finances about one-third of the recurrent budget and almost all public investment. Structural adjustment borrowing from the IFIs after 1985 resulted in the escalation of external debt from US$1.5 billion in 1982 to nearly US$9 billion in December 1998. Tanzania has qualified for debt relief under the revised HIPC2, through which debt relief will be conditional on enhanced anti-poverty programmes.

Concern with the apparent inability of aid to spur rapid or sustained policy change has led donors to reconsider their overall approach to development cooperation (Partnership Africa, 1997; World Bank, 1998; UK, DFID, 1999; Helleiner,

1999; Lancaster, 1999). The key elements in the new approach are partnership, local ownership and sustainability.

Substantive areas of concern for development agencies in Tanzania reflect the global development agenda: growth with equity (including gender and anti-poverty programmes), priority investment in social capital (with agreed goals for basic health and education), democracy and good governance (including anti-corruption), and environmental protection.

Inevitably, aid donors hugely influence the policy-reform process, and the ownership issue thus boils down to the government 'owning' a largely external agenda. Implementation of ambitious reforms, in particular the decentralization of local government, is slowed down by the general non-involvement of local policy-makers in the implementation process (Therkildsen, 1999).

Poverty, inequality & social development

Tanzania is among the poorest countries in the world, with approximately half the population (and proportionately more in rural areas) earning incomes insufficient to guarantee a minimum level of nutrition and basic standard of living (World Bank, 1993). Tanzania ranks in the bottom 10 per cent of UNDP's Human Development Index.

Attempts to identify trends in the incidence and distribution of poverty over the years have yielded inconclusive results. In a recent rural survey, nearly twice as many respondents said that life had deteriorated for their household over the previous decade as said things had improved (37 per cent compared with 21 per cent).

Recent poverty research using participatory methods produced similar results concerning poverty and its principal causes (Narayan, 1997). Poverty was associated with the availability of fertile land, family size, education, income from cash crops and access to all-weather roads. Small, fragmented plots, hand-hoe technology and limited access to credit and

101

agricultural inputs keep most farming households at or below the poverty line, with seasonal food shortages common. Female-headed households are generally poorer than those headed by men. Factors affecting women's poverty are lack of capital assets, including land, social exclusion and vulnerability (*ibid.*: 35).

Recent research draws attention to the diversification of sources of rural income, including casual agricultural labour, petty trade, fishing and artisanal mining. The government's target is to eliminate absolute poverty by the year 2025 and to reduce it to half its current level by 2010 (URT, Vice-President's Office, 1998: 20).

Trends in educational inequalities are discussed below (Havnevik and Harsmar, 1999).

Opportunities & constraints in the present policy regime

Starting from a position where, less than two decades ago, the state barely tolerated private business, it is not surprising that there is still significant opposition in Tanzania to the ideology of market-led development. It does not help that foreign investors and the Asian business community are widely perceived to be the major beneficiaries of the new policy regime. Although the government frequently reiterates its commitment to a market economy, actions frequently reveal another, deeper-rooted tendency favouring state ownership, limits on foreign investment and widespread discretionary controls of business activities by regional and district authorities.

Research on the regulatory environment controlling investment shows Tanzania in a very poor light compared with other African countries. The amount of red tape faced by investors and the related frequency of 'rent-seeking' are significantly greater in Tanzania than, for example, in Namibia,

Uganda or Ghana (Coopers and Lybrand, 1996). The IMF estimates that sustained real growth of 6–7 per cent per capita is required to keep up with the expected increase in Africa's labour force; 8–9 per cent would allow Africa to attain half the current income of the industrial countries within a generation (Ouattara, 1999). Tanzania's most promising growth poles – mining and tourism – are unlikely to create much direct employment, and small- to medium-scale agriculture remains the best bet in this regard.

In summary, major opportunities include the following: good financial discipline and sustainable inflation rate; positive growth in GDP; improvements in tax collection; important revenue prospects from mineral investments; reduced debt burden under HIPC2; continued donor confidence; and continued political stability.

Nevertheless, there are serious constraints. Despite major reforms, the quality of official social services has yet to improve, levels of government transparency and accountability remain low, poverty and youth unemployment continue to be pervasive and agricultural export prices remain depressed.

Trends in education

Once considered an appropriate and progressive model for poor third-world countries to emulate, Tanzania's education system has more recently been singled out for its serious quantitative and qualitative shortcomings. Whereas in the 1960s and 1970s, education policy tried heroically, but unsuccessfully, to reorient school curricula towards the needs of a poor and largely rural society, in the 1980s and 1990s the stress has shifted towards preparing Tanzanians for the challenges of the twenty-first century in science and technology, computers and the internet. If the early, inward-looking, policy objectives could not be met, we should not underestimate the magnitude of the challenges posed by liberalization and globalization.

Education accounted for 27 per cent of total government

103

Mkapa on education

'We cannot talk of improving higher education without addressing weaknesses in primary and secondary school education. ... Above all there must be developed an interest and capacity in the sciences at lower levels, including among girls and disadvantaged groups, without which we should not expect miracles at the university level. This calls for a studied commitment to universal primary education and a planned increased intake at secondary school level.'

President Benjamin Mkapa, opening address to the sixth Conference of Rectors, Vice Chancellors and Presidents of African Universities, Arusha, February 1999.

spending in 1994, falling to 24 per cent in 1998. Salaries account for 96 per cent of primary education expenditures, leaving little or nothing for 'other charges' (URT, MOEC, 1996: 7–8). Partly as a result, parental contributions to the cost of primary schooling have risen steadily over the years, but parents do not consider they are getting value for money (TADREG, 1997a, 1997b). The government has launched an ambitious education sector development programme (SDP) with support from major donor agencies. The SDP seeks to increase enrolments to achieve universal primary education by 2015, while at the same time reversing the declining quality of primary schooling. Private participation in educational provision is encouraged at all levels (URT, MOEC, 1999a). The success of the SDP depends in part on the implementation of the current decentralization policy, through which local governments and communities will have much greater freedom than currently to manage social services, including hiring and firing personnel. Critics consider the programme too ambitious, too costly (US$375 million), lacking in local ownership and political commitment, and vulnerable to donor disunity.

To date, the SDP does not include post-secondary education,

though the MSTHE is preparing a plan for this sector to be included in the SDP.

After some years of rapid expansion in the late 1970s, primary school enrolments stagnated and were actually lower in absolute terms in 1988 than a decade earlier (URT, MOEC, 1991: 23). Net primary school enrolment rates (proportion of 7–13-year-olds in school) were 57 per cent in 1998 compared with 67 per cent a decade earlier ((TADREG, 1998; MOEC, 1999a). Only one-third of 7–9-year-olds are in school, rising to over 80 per cent of 10–14-year-olds.

Primary school enrolments increased by 19 per cent between 1990 and 1998, considerably less than the increase in the school-age population. If the enrolment figures are correct, the positive trend in the net enrolment rate from 1990 to 1998 is questionable. MOEC indicates a small net drop in primary enrolments between 1997 and 1998 (URT, MOEC, 1999a: 7).

Secondary enrolments grew by more than half (56 per cent) between 1990 and 1998, with all the increase taking place in the state sector. Private-school enrolments actually fell during this period. Despite recent net growth, secondary enrolment rates in Tanzania are still among the lowest in Africa and the world.

Urban–rural and district-level inequalities in primary educational inputs and outputs are significant, despite official policies aimed at equity. On a combined index based on enrolment rates, proportion of Grade A teachers, pupil–teacher ratios, class size and school-leaving examination results, eight of the top ten districts are regional headquarters (TADREG, 1998: Table 4).

Gender inequalities in schooling increase from the primary level upwards. Girls' performance is significantly below boys' at the primary school-leaving examination, particularly in maths, as well as at 'O' (Form 4) and 'A' levels (Form 6) (TADREG, 1990).

105

There is some evidence that social inequalities in school selection have increased over time. In a large sample of Form 4 students in 1980, Malekela (1983) found that 57 per cent had fathers who were farmers, compared with only 36 per cent of a sample taken ten years later.

The growth of private secondary schooling in the 1980s led to growing spatial inequalities in educational opportunities. By 1990, five of the 20 mainland regions accounted for 60 per cent of all private schools and the bottom 12 regions only 24 per cent. A fifth of all private secondary schools are in the Kilimanjaro Region (URT, MOEC, 1999a: 43). There is a religious dimension to private school inequalities. By 1992, nearly half of private secondary schools were run by Christian churches, whereas only 6 per cent were run by the official Muslim school body (Cooksey et al., 1994: 225).

Income and other inequalities in Tanzania are likely to influence the social demand for education at different levels.

Trends in employment

Economic liberalization in the last 15 years or so has led to the rapid informalization of the urban and rural economy. The informal sector is said to account for 60 per cent of non-agricultural employment and value added in informal manufacturing, commerce and personal services is thought to exceed that generated in the formal sector (Dar, 1995). Tripp (1988) found informal-sector incomes to be more than six times the average wage of formal sector workers.

The most recent available data show male workers in the government sector earning on average 20 per cent more than men in the private sector and women 50 per cent more (Dar, 1995). Parastatal pay was better than that of government. The monthly wage of a male graduate was three times that of an uneducated male; for females the ratio was nine times greater.

Given that public secondary and higher education has been

highly subsidized, it is not surprising that the private returns to post-primary education are positive. For male and female graduates respectively, private rates of return were 9.9 per cent and 11.4 per cent per annum. However, the high public cost of university education produces a significantly negative social rate of return: –5.7 per cent compared with +2.8 per cent for sub-Saharan Africa as a whole. This means that 'the economic cost of providing this education is greater than the net present value of economic benefits' (Dar, 1995: 14). This astonishing, albeit dated, conclusion remains to be refuted or confirmed by the manpower survey due in late 2000.[1]

The Labour Force Survey found 42 per cent of formal sector workers in the civil service, 23 per cent in parastatal companies and 35 per cent in the private sector. The retrenchment of civil servants, privatization and closure of parastatals, and (perhaps) growing investment in the private sector will probably lead to a rapid change in these relative proportions.

Estimates of unemployment vary considerably. The government's New Employment Policy (1995) cites an overall unemployment rate of 13 per cent. Unemployment in the 15–19 age group was said to be close to 40 per cent in urban areas (Dar, 1995: 17). The end of guaranteed employment in the state sector and the continued slow growth of the formal economy may have ushered in a period of growing unemployment among the more educated. Certainly there is plenty of anecdotal evidence to this effect, particularly among arts and social science graduates.

Note

1 A manpower (labour force) survey was undertaken in 2000/01 but its results have not yet been published (2000/01 Integrated Labour Force Survey of Tanzania Mainland).

References

University of Dar es Salaam documents*

2000a. *1999 Progress and Financial Reports for Individual Programmes/Projects and Workplans for 2000*. Annual Review meeting for 1999 Activities, Doc. 1.

2000b. *Annual Progress Review of SIDA/SAREC Projects as of December 31, 1999.*

1994. *Appraisals, Studies, Reports. Reference Documentation*, Issue No. 3.

1995a. *Action Plan and Progress Report.*

2000c. *Conceptual Notes on the Proposed Activities for the 2001–2003 Agreement Period, UDSM-SIDA/SAREC Cooperation 2001–2003.* Annual Review Meeting for 1999 Activities, Doc. 3.

1993. *Corporate Strategic Plan*, No. 3.

1995–. *Facts and Figures*. Annually since 1995.

1989. *Financial Regulations.*

1999. *Five-Year Rolling Strategic Plans of Colleges, Faculties and Institutes.*

1995. *Income-Generating Measures*. Vol. III.

1999b.'The New Organizational Structure of the University of Dar es Salaam'.

1999a. *Report of 1998 UDSM Academic Audit.*

1998. *Research Policy and Operational Procedures for the UDSM.*

Planning Unit. 1994. *Towards the Establishment of Management Information System (MIS) at the University of Dar es Salaam.*

Faculty of Education. 1999. *Proceedings of the Educational Research Dissemination Workshop*. Morogoro.

—— 2000. *Report on the Conceptual Conference on Basic Education Renewal Research Initiative for Poverty Alleviation*. Arusha.

Faculty of Engineering. 1985. *Graduate and Employment Survey*. Dar es Salaam: University of Dar es Salaam.

—— 1989. *University Education and the Engineering Profession in Tanzania, Results of Graduates' and Employers' Survey 1989.*

—— 1995. *National Level Impact Study 1995, Final Report.*

—— 1998. *Tracer Study for Graduates, Instructor Trainees and Employers, Final Report.*

Institutional Transformation Programme

1993. *Institutional Transformation Program 'UDSM 2000' – Draft Framework and Call for Contributions*. Parts A to F.

1994. *Institutional Transformation Programme 'UDSM 2000'.*

1995. *Institutional Transformation Program.*

1993. *Proceedings of the 1st Annual Consultative Meeting.*

1995. *Proceedings of the 2nd Annual Consultative Meeting.*

---

* Place of publication is Dar es Salaam unless otherwise noted.

1996. *Proceedings of the 3rd Annual Consultative Meeting.*

1998. *Proceedings of the 4th Annual Consultative Meeting.*

1999. *Proceedings of the 6th Annual Consultative Workshop on the UDSM Transformation Programme.*

1995. *Proceedings of the Seminar on Effective Communication for Senior Administrative Staff.*

1993. *Programme Outline, Report and Plan of Action,* Issue no. 3.

1997. *Progress Report as at January 1997.*

1999a. *Proposed Priority Future Support Areas for UDSM.*

1999b. *Proposed Organizational Structure of the University of Dar es Salaam.*

1998. *Research Policy and Operational Procedures for the UDSM.*

1996. *University-level Five-Year Rolling Strategic Plan, 1996–2001.*

1997. *University-level Five-Year Rolling Strategic Plan, 1997–2002.*

1999. *University-level Five-Year Rolling Strategic Plan for 1999/2000–2003/ 2004.*

Other University of Dar es Salaam sources

Bali, B.K.C. 1989. 'Project Proposal for Computerization of Administrative Functions at the UDSM Central Administration'.

Chungu, A. 2000. 'Income Diversification and Financial Sustainability: Lessons from the UDSM Transformation Programme'. Paper presented at Conference on Financial Sustainability in Higher Education in Southern Africa, University of Cape Town, South Africa, 11–13 March.

Ishumi, Abel, Sam Maghimbi and Willy Kalembo. 2000. 'The Need for Expansion of Student Enrolment at UDSM: With Special Reference to Privately Sponsored Students'. Paper presented at 7th Annual Consultative Workshop on UDSM Transformation Programme, Dar es Salaam.

Kaijage, Erasmus. 2000. *Faculty of Commerce and Management Graduates and their Employees: A Tracer Study.* Business and Management Research Series No. 2. Dar es Salaam: University of Dar es Salaam Faculty of Commerce and Management.

——. 2001. 'Institutional Transformation Programme of the University of Dar es Salaam-UDSM 2000'. *Dawasa Newsletter* (special edition, March): 2–7.

Luhanga, Matthew. 1999. 'Briefing on the opening of the UDSM Computer Centre building'. Unpublished, 28 September.

Luhanga, M.L. and T.S.A. Mbwette. 1998. 'University Education in Tanzania: A Perspective for the 21st Century, UDSM Experiences', in *Proceedings of the Workshop for Members of Parliament.*

Lwambuka, L. and Beda Mutagahywa. 1993. *Tracer Study for the Graduates, Instructor Trainees and Employers, Final Report.* Faculty of Engineering.

Mannatte, P.L. 1991. *Report on the Computation of the University of Dar es*

Salaam Unit Costs, Planning Office.

Masuha, J.R. et al. 1993. *Report of the Task Force on Amendments to the University of Dar es Salaam Act 1970.*

Materu, P.N. 1993. *Report of the Follow-up Committee on Additional Ways of Funding the UDSM. Practical Actions.*

Materu, P.N., T.A.S. Mbwette and R.R. Sauer. 1996. 'The "UDSM-2000" Institutional Transformation Programme at the University of Dar es Salaam: Concept, Status, Experiences and Perspective for the Future'. Report Prepared for Donors to African Education/Working Group on Higher Education. Durban.

Mgaya, Y.D., S.K. Shija, B. Kundi and M. Meshack. 1999. 'Five Years of the UDSM Transformation Programme 1994–1998'. Paper presented at Annual Consultative Workshop on the UDSM Transformation Programme. Dar es Salaam, University of Dar es Salaam.

Mkude, D.J. 1998. 'Students' Role in the Transformation of Higher Education Institutions'. Paper presented at the Southern African Association for Institutional Research Conference (SAAIR). Cape Town.

Muhimbili University College of Health Sciences (MUCHS). *Research Bulletin,* 1995 and various years.

———. 1995. *Research Policy.*

———. 1999. *Five-Year Strategic Rolling Plans, 1998/2003.*

Mutagahywa, Beda and J.K. Bakari. 2000. 'Status of Information and Communication Technology at the University of Dar es Salaam, Computing Centre'.

UDASA. 1994. *Report on Institutional Transformation Programme of the University of Dar es Salaam – UDSM 2000.*

———. 1997. 'Ad hoc Committee Report on "UDSM 2000"'. Unpublished mimeo.

Sokoine University of Agriculture (SUA)

Chambo, Suleman and Brian Cooksey. 2000. 'The Changing Form of Tanzanian Agricultural Cooperatives under Market Liberalization'. Paper presented to REPOA Research Workshop, Whitesands Hotel, Dar es Salaam.

SUA. 1997. *Corporate Strategic Plan to the Year 2005 and Beyond (Objectives and Strategies).* Morogoro.

———. 1999. *Prospectus 1999/2000.* Morogoro.

———. 2000a. *Research Policy, Priority Areas and Guidelines.* Morogoro.

———. 2000b. *Corporate Strategic Plan Implementation, Progress Report July 1998–March 2000.* Morogoro.

———. 2000c. SUACONSULT. *Proposed Operational Policy and Procedures for Consultancy Services, Short Courses, Tailor Made Programmes and Contract Research.* Morogoro.

Other sources

Abegaz, Berhanu and Lisbeth Levey. 1996. *What Price Information? Priority Setting in African Universities*. Washington, DC: American Association for the Advancement of Science.

Ajayi, J.F. Ade et al. 1996. *The African Experience with Higher Education*. Columbus, OH: Ohio University Press.

Alberts, Tom and Marcelo Dougnac, 2000. *Sida Supported Environmental Research Projects in Tanzania*, Stockholm: SIDA.

Association of African Universities. 1991. *Study on Cost Effectiveness and Efficiency in African Universities. A Synthesis Report*. Accra: AAU.

Avenstrup, R. and Patti Swarts. 2000. 'Report of the NUFU evaluation mission in Tanzania'. Dar es Salaam. Draft.

Bgoya, Walter. 1995. 'A survey of the human rights situation in Tanzania'. Dar es Salaam.

Coopers & Lybrand.1996. *The Investor Roadmap to Tanzania*. Washington: Economic Growth Center.

Committee of Vice-Chancellors and Principals in Tanzania. 1996. 'The Need to Increase Funding for Tanzanian Universities'. Paper submitted to MSTHE.

——. 1997. *Public Universities Remaining Competitive under Liberalised Educational Environment in Tanzania*.

Cooksey, Brian et al. 1991. *Teachers' Living and Working Conditions in Tanzania*. Dar es Salaam: SIDA/World Bank.

Cooksey, Brian, David Court and Ben Makau. 1994. 'Education for Self-Reliance and *Harambee*', in Joel Barkan (ed.), *Beyond Capitalism vs Socialism in Kenya and Tanzania*. Nairobi: East African Educational Publishers.

Cooksey, Brian and Sibylle Riedmiller. 1997. 'Tanzanian Education in the 'Nineties: beyond the diploma disease'. *Assessment in Education* 4, 1: 121–35.

Court, David. 1975. 'The Experience of Higher Education in East Africa: The University of Dar es Salaam as a New Model?', *Comparative Education* 11, 3, October: 193–218.

——. 1980. 'The Development Ideal in Higher Education: The Experience of Kenya and Tanzania'. *Higher Education* 9: 657–80.

Dar, A. 1995. 'Labour Markets in Tanzania'. Poverty and Social Policy Department. Washington, DC: World Bank.

Embassy of Sweden. *Semi-Annual Report Tanzania*. Dar es Salaam, March 1995.

Farrant, J. 1997. *Evaluation of UDSM Strategic Planning*. London: Universitas Higher Education Management Consultants.

Havnevik, Kjell and Mats Harsmar. 1999. *The Diversified Future: An Institutional Approach to Rural Development in Tanzania*. Stockholm: Ministry of Foreign Affairs.

Helleiner, Gerry. 1999. 'The Legacies of Julius Nyerere: An Economist's

Reflections'. Paper presented to meeting of the Consultative Group for Tanzania on Changing Aid Relationships in Tanzania, University of Toronto, Toronto.

International Cooperative Alliance. 1999. *Tanzania Cooperative Country Study.* Geneva.

Kelly, Kevin. 2000. 'East African Human Rights Record "Poor"'. *The East African,* 6-12 March: 5.

Lancaster, Carol. 1999. *Aid to Africa: So Much to Do, So Little Done.* Chicago: University of Chicago Press.

Lang, Ulrika. 1998. 'Trade unions in transition'. Dar es Salaam: SIDA. Draft.

Macha, P. S. 1979. 'Ad Hoc Committee on Improving Communication among University Organs'. University of Dar es Salaam Council Report. Dar es Salaam: UDSM.

Malekela, George. 1983. 'Access to Secondary Education in Sub-Saharan Africa: The Tanzanian Experiment'. PhD dissertation, University of Chicago.

Masabo, Tumbo. 2000. 'Comments on Chachage', University of Dar es Salaam *Academic Staff Assembly Newsletter.* March.

Narayan, Deepa. 1997. *Voices of the Poor: Poverty and Social Capital in Tanzania.* Washington, DC: World Bank.

Ngirwa, C.A. 2000. 'Main Features of the New Operational Policy and Procedures on Human Resources Management at the University of Dar es Salaam'. UDSM Councillors Workshop on UDSM Transformation Programme, Sheraton Hotel, Dar es Salaam, 19 August.

Open University of Tanzania (OUT). 1999. *Newsletter* 1: 1.

Ouattara, Alassane. 1999. 'Africa: An Agenda for the 21st Century,' *Finance and Development,* March.

Partnership Africa/Ministry of Foreign Affairs. 1997. *Partnership with Africa.* Stockholm.

Penrose, Perran. 1997. 'Cost Sharing in Education'. Draft.

Peter, Chris, Haroub Othmann, Mwemezi Mukoyogo, Walter Bgoya, Matilda Philip and Sanne Olsen. 1995. *Human Rights, Political and Legal Legitimacy-Strategy for Danish Development Cooperation Programme.* Dar es Salaam: DANIDA.

Saint, William. 1992. *Universities in Africa: Strategies for Stabilization and Revitalization.* The World Bank Technical Paper No. 194, Africa Technical Department Series. Washington, DC: World Bank.

Sanyal, Bikas and Michael Kinunda. 1977. *Higher Education for Self-reliance: the Tanzanian Experience.* Paris: International Institute for Educational Planning.

Shivji, Issa. 1993. 'The Democracy Debate in Africa: Tanzania', *Review of African Political Economy,* 50.

Swedish International Development Cooperation Agency (SIDA). 1998. *A Sea of Opportunities, Research Cooperation in 1998.* Stockholm: Department

112